PRAISE FOR GRACE ~~...~~

"Nicki Dechert Carlson will reach right into
your heart and mind through her book, *Grace-faced*.
Every chapter is personal, practical, and hopeful.
If you long to unlock God's perspective on your life,
you need to read this book!"
—Debbie Taylor Williams, author of
Pray with Purpose, Live with Passion, and
The Plan A Woman in a Plan B World—

"In *Grace-faced*, Nicki Dechert Carlson tackles important
spiritual issues in a conversational, 'sit around the
campfire' manner, while still delivering a powerful and
compelling Christ-centered message. Her writing is
personal and appealing. She truly hits the mark as she
deftly deals with human grief, failure, faith, grace, self-
awareness and redemption with the perfect touch of
playful humor that keeps the reader engaged as they
dig into these often solemn and weighty topics.
Nicki has crafted a book that will undoubtedly serve as
a welcomed salve for many experiencing the pain, fear,
worry or questions that sometimes obscure our heaven-
centered vision. Bravo!"
—Scott Delaney, Award-Winning Christian
Fiction Author of *The Global Calling* Series—

"If you are looking for your next inspiring read,
you've found it! Nicki's humorous anecdotes and heart-
felt, spiritual messages encourage us to seek God's
perspective in every situation. You will want to be
grace-faced, too!"
—Keri Wilt, Motivational Speaker, Writer, and
Great-Great-Granddaughter of Frances Hodgson
Burnett, author of *The Secret Garden*—

NICKI DECHERT CARLSON

GRACE~FACED

Pursuing the Life-Changing
Perspective of a Loving God

XULON PRESS ELITE

Xulon Press
2301 Lucien Way #415
Maitland, FL 32751
407.339.4217
www.xulonpress.com

Paperback ISBN-13: 978-1-6628-3084-6
Hard Cover ISBN-13: 978-1-6628-3085-3
Ebook ISBN-13: 978-1-6628-3086-0

For my husband, John.
There would be no "me,"
if it weren't for you.

TABLE OF CONTENTS

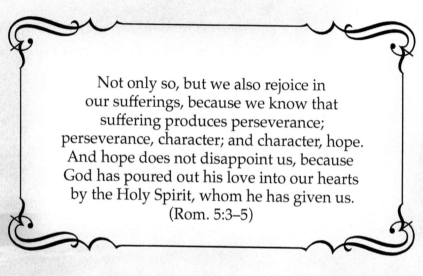

Not only so, but we also rejoice in
our sufferings, because we know that
suffering produces perseverance;
perseverance, character; and character, hope.
And hope does not disappoint us, because
God has poured out his love into our hearts
by the Holy Spirit, whom he has given us.
(Rom. 5:3–5)

INTRODUCTION

Look to the Lord and his strength; seek his face always.
(1 Chron. 16:11)

I'm from the South. I remember numerous times my mama or one of her sweet friends sat across from me while I had a "coming apart," meaning an emotional breakdown of various sorts. These strong women would listen while I cried and then offer wisdom and advice. As the tears slowed, they would inevitably give me a hug, wipe the tears from my cheeks, and say, "Now, go fix your face and you'll feel better."

"Fix your face" meant go to the bathroom, splash some cool water on your face, and then pat it dry. "Fix your face" meant wipe away the smeared eye makeup and apply some concealer to mask the red puffy places, and maybe swipe on some fresh lipstick. "Fix your face" meant it was time to change your perspective and get back to the business of living life.

It's not always easy to fix our faces. It's hard when all manner of suffering comes our way. It's hard when that suffering becomes a test of endurance. It's hard when trials require us to do the hard work of becoming more faithful and well-rounded people. It's hard when clinging to hope feels counter-intuitive. But that's exactly what God asks us to do. He wants us to fix our face on Him.

> *Not only so, but we also rejoice in our sufferings, because we know that suffering produces perseverance; perseverance, character; and character, hope. And hope does not disappoint us, because God has poured out his love into our hearts by the Holy Spirit, whom he has given us.*
> *(Rom. 5:3–5)*

Personal growth doesn't occur without effort and difficulty (suffering), without commitment (perseverance), without change (character development), or without belief (hope). This book will take us on that four-tiered journey. With short, easy-to-read —and often humorous —chapters, we will learn to stop in the midst of life's many problems and turn to seek God's perspective on them. We will embrace His character and start to look, think, and act more like Jesus.

One of my favorite passages in the Bible can be found in the book of Exodus. God appointed Moses as His interpreter and mouthpiece to give warning, instruction, and advice to His people. Moses entered the Lord's presence on the top of a mountain, fasting there for forty days and nights.

> *When Moses came down from Mount Sinai with the two tablets of the covenant law in his hands, he was not aware that his face was radiant because he had spoken with the LORD.*
> *(Exod. 34:29)*

Talk about a fixed face. Talk about a facelift! I love knowing we can't leave the presence of God unchanged.

We are not the same coming out as we are going in. God's perspective changes everything.

Hannah, wife of Elkanah, gives us a perfect example of this; she, too, experienced a changed face after spending time with God. Hannah prayed so fervently and wept so bitterly before the Lord at the temple, that the priest, Eli, accused her of being drunk.

"Not so, my lord," Hannah replied, "I am a woman who is
deeply troubled. I have not been drinking wine or beer; I was
pouring out my soul to the LORD."
(1 Sam. 1:15)

The Scripture goes on to say that when Hannah returned home, her countenance was sad no longer (v. 18).

A good friend of mine taught me that a person's countenance is the sum of his or her entire being and personality, wrapped up in the image of his or her face. You can learn a lot about a person from just his or her face. Wrinkles around my eyes speak to a life of laughter and tears, scattered freckles speak to years of playing tennis in the sun, and my bulbous nose and light-colored eyes speak to my ancestry.

Likewise, we can discover a great deal about our heavenly Father by looking into *His* face. When we spend time with God, we find a heavenly Father who cares about every detail of the lives we lead. His love for us is so great that He never stops trying to woo us into a deeper relationship with Him. We only need to pause long enough to recognize His extraordinary efforts, draw near to Him, and yield to His development of spiritual fruit in our lives. It stands to reason, then, that how we see God's countenance dictates how we respond to Him.

When we seek God's face (by seeking to intimately know Him) and not just seek His hands (by only coming to him with our requests), we experience a changed perspective and a shift in the way we live our lives. We begin to see His pursuing love at work all around us, and we eagerly desire to join Him in that work. Like Moses coming down from the mountaintop and Hannah returning home from the temple, we find ourselves awash in His glory, our countenances radiant. When we turn to face God and fix our eyes on Him, our own faces change in the light of his love and mercy. *In other words, we become grace-faced.*

Suffering

Not only so, but we also glory in our sufferings
(Rom. 5:3a)

FACING SUFFERING

I have told you these things, so that in me you may have peace. In this world you will have trouble. But take heart! I have overcome the world.
(John 16:33)

Jesus never promised ease. He knew the world was full of sin and its consequences. We will suffer. Life will be hard. The good news is that we can do hard things because Jesus Christ sent His spirit to live inside us and help us. He already did the hardest thing imaginable when He suffered the crucifixion; better still, He did it on our behalf. The victory belongs to Jesus, and if we belong to Him, God promises the victory is ours as well.

If we turn to face God in our suffering, we can do more than just *survive*; we can *thrive*. How? By seeking His face and not just His hands; that means, we must explore who God really is and not just ask Him to meet our wants and needs. What does God want to teach us through these tribulations? What is He trying to reveal about Himself? Not only can we weather difficult storms, but we can safely arrive on new shores with greater strength and wisdom because of our arduous journeys.

In addition to victory, God promises to remain with us during troublesome times. No matter how terrible life may seem, nothing we experience here can snatch us away from Him. And His presence? It changes everything.

Who shall separate us from the love of Christ? Shall trouble or hardship or persecution or famine or nakedness or danger or sword? As it is written: "For your sake we face death all day long; we are considered as sheep to be slaughtered." No, in all these things we are more than conquerors through him who loved us. For I am convinced that neither death nor life, neither angels nor demons, neither the present nor the future, nor any powers, neither height nor depth, nor anything else in all creation, will be able to separate us from the love of God that is in Christ Jesus our Lord.
(Rom. 8:35–39)

With God's help, we can turn our complaining into praise, our fears into faith, our moaning into rejoicing, and our greatest struggle into our greatest testimony of victory for God.

Dear God,
Thank you for standing with us in dark times. May we seek You for solace and aid because You are a good, loving Father. Help us to learn the lessons You long to teach us and to find new depths of intimacy with You in these valleys. Let us look to Jesus for comfort and understanding because He endured ultimate suffering on our behalf. May we bask in Your grace as we turn to face You in our own suffering.
In the powerful name of Jesus Christ, Amen.

Additional verses to read about suffering:
1 Peter 5:10
2 Corinthians 1:3–4
Psalm 34:19
2 Corinthians 4:16–18
Romans 8:18
1 Peter 3:14
Philippians 1:29
2 Corinthians 1:5

FACING GRIEF

So I'll sing Hallelujah,
You were an angel in the shape of my mum.
When I fell down you were there holding me up.
Spread your wings as you go,
And when God takes you back
He'll say, "Hallelujah, you're home."[1]
—"Supermarket Flowers" by Ed Sheeran

This morning I did not want to get out of bed. My alarm on weekdays is set for the last possible minute I can wake and still accomplish what needs to be done. Normally, I wake up earlier than the alarm due to the sounds of my husband getting ready. But this morning, I kept going back to sleep. The first words out of my mouth were, "I have *zero* get-up-and-go today!" My sweet husband gave me extra hugs, which always helps. I threw on some clothes and headed to the kitchen for that heavenly concoction called coffee, but still, all I wanted to do was crawl back under the covers of my comfy bed and hibernate. I'd had a great night of sleep, so my lethargy remained a mystery.

I got my youngest off to school, came back home, warmed up the remainder of that merciful cup of coffee, and turned on my phone. That's when it dawned on me. It was February 28, an annually-dreaded day for me. Somehow my body knew the date, even before it registered with my conscious mind and heart. Every year, this day comes, and every year, I'm reminded of losing my mom to cancer when I was fifteen years old. I have now lived quite a bit longer on this earth without her than I ever did with her, yet her influence on me somehow continues to grow year after year.

Death. Just saying the word feels like a sucker punch to the gut. All the platitudes in the world cannot assuage the heaviness of grief, despite it being a very common, shared experience. We will all lose loved ones. We will all die. It's inevitable. So why is this still so hard?

Maybe if we could get a really good look at what's waiting for us in heaven, in the *after*life, in this other realm happening in and around us, we could better understand. But we're not privy to that. We possess a very limited, myopic view. This life. Here and now. Tangible experiences. It's no wonder the matters of death and afterlife exist a little beyond our comprehension.

When people ask me for advice on handling the death of a loved one, I always tell them two things. First, you can't "not do" grief. Grief is living and active. It will not be ignored forever. You can't escape it. You can't go around it, under it, or over it. You have to go *through* it. Avoidance will only complicate the experience and make it so much harder in the long-run. The second thing I tell people is this: don't censor yourself. When traveling the road through the dark valley of grief, just do you. Be yourself in all your glory and all your ugly. Judging yourself for feelings is pointless. I tell my son almost daily, "Feelings are okay. They're just feelings. They're not good or bad. It's how you *act* on feelings that matters." It is so easy to get caught in the trappings of judging our own feelings. Beware of thoughts like these:

I shouldn't feel this way.
Why can't I just be happy again?
I shouldn't laugh because I'm supposed to be mourning.
I have to get myself together. I'm bawling in the middle of the grocery store.
I haven't cried at all. What is wrong with me?

Everyone processes grief differently. No two experiences are exactly alike because no two people are exactly alike. To get through grief, you have to give yourself permission to *feel* all the *feelings*. It will probably be good, bad, and ugly. And that's okay. There may be times when you need a full-on ugly cry for what seems like a completely unfounded reason. There may be times when you are physically aching from sadness, then hear something funny and laugh so hard you fall out of a chair. For me, it was a crazy roller coaster of ups and downs and hairpin turns that came without warning. But there was an intimacy with God on that ride—and with the friends and family who climbed into the seats nearest me—that I treasure in the deepest, truest parts of my soul.

Being with God amidst the throes of grief and really truly spending time connecting with Him is not easy. In fact, it can be downright painful. I know I censored my prayers because good little Christian girls weren't supposed to be angry with God. So I said appropriate, churchy things, but inside I felt super-ticked-off. Devastated, even. A mentor at church said something to me that I will never forget, about talking to God when you're angry at Him. She said, "You think God doesn't already know you're mad at Him? God knows how you feel! You can't possibly tell Him something He doesn't already know. So just talk to Him already." Huh. Just talk to Him. Like a friend. Like someone you trust to love you despite your crazy feelings. Novel idea. It was freeing for me, realizing that I could just be my train-wreck-of-a-person self with the God of the universe. I realized God could more than handle my anger, my unfathomable disappointment, and my grief, even when I directed it straight at Him. After all, didn't I believe God could handle anything?

> You lay it on Jesus—all of it. Not only can He handle it; He *wants* it.

So here is what you do, friends. You lay it on Jesus—all of it. Not only can He handle it; He *wants* it.

> *Cast all your anxiety on Him because He cares for you.*
> *(1 Pet. 5:7)*

Now, let's talk about the blame game, because no conversation about grief is complete without it. Death, as we all know, was not in the original plan. It only entered the world after Adam and Eve's fall from grace, which necessitated the ultimate sacrifice of Jesus to cover up all that sin (and death) so we can be holy (and sinless) enough to enter the presence of a perfect God.

Knowing all this led to some pretty hefty questions on my part, though. Did God kill my mom? Did He give her cancer as a test of her faith and she failed? Did I not have enough faith or not pray hard enough, so He chose not to heal her? Did He need her more than I did, so He took her to heaven to be with Him? Did He just need another angel and chose her? No, no, and no. My mom died because she was human. Death, ever since that first bite of forbidden fruit, is now an inescapable part of life. God knows this, and this is why He had a plan named Jesus from the very beginning.

This is how much God loved the world: He gave his Son, his one and only Son. And this is why: so that no one need be destroyed; by believing in him, anyone can have a whole and lasting life. God didn't go to all the trouble of sending his Son merely to point an accusing finger, telling the world how bad it was. He came to help, to put the world right again. Anyone who trusts in him is acquitted; anyone who refuses to trust him has long since been under the death sentence without knowing it. And why? Because of that person's failure to believe in the one-of-a-kind Son of God when introduced to him.
(John 3:16–18, MSG)

Such an amazing, incomprehensible love our Heavenly Father has for us. His heart breaks when ours does. A sweet friend of my mother advised me after my mama died to look around at all the people offering support and encouragement. She told me to embrace every hug, every smile, read every card, and smell every flower because all were gifts straight from the Lord. How does God love us and comfort us in the wake of death? Through the people around us. That hug from a friend? A hug from the Lord. That meal the neighbor brought over? Prepared at the prompting of the Lord. Grieve with open arms, not clenched fists. You're not alone. Jesus has walked this dark road too, and He's walking yours right alongside you.

> Grieve with open arms, not clenched fists.

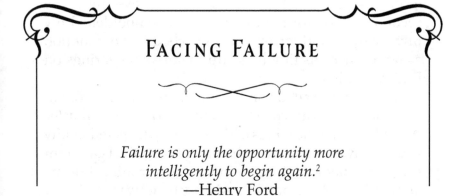

FACING FAILURE

Failure is only the opportunity more
intelligently to begin again.[2]
—Henry Ford

It was a beautiful Sunday morning. I sat four rows from the front of the church with my clean, groomed, and finely dressed children surrounding me. My husband, John, was leading worship on the stage in front of us, playing a moving song of praise on his guitar while singing.

My youngest was two years old, and he had lost interest in the service. He desperately wanted to roll around on the floor in front of our seats and talk loudly to himself while playing make-believe games. He squirmed. I put a hand on his knee. He squirmed and talked. I squeezed his knee. He yanked his knee away. He decided this was a good time to talk louder, while looking directly at me. I started to put my arm around him to pull him into my lap, so he ducked away from my arm, slid out of his chair, and bolted down the row, up the aisle, through the side door, up the stage stairs, and launched himself at his father. In the middle of the worship song, the youngest of the Carlson children quickly wrapped his hands, arms, legs, and feet monkey-style around his father's leg.

I sat completely stunned at the spectacle in front of me. What do I do? Do I leave him there and let his dad finish the song and then deal with him? Will it be even more disruptive if I go on stage to retrieve him? The seconds it took for me to decide only emboldened my tiny two-year-old terror, and I watched in slow-motion as he reached his tiny hand up to stroke the strings on Daddy's guitar.

I sprang into action and made my way to the front of the room with as much dignity and calm as I could muster. When I reached the wings of the stage, I whispered loudly and angrily at my son from behind the curtain. I gave him my most maternal "you're in so much trouble, buddy" face, but it yielded nothing. My husband was staring at me with a horrified look that pleaded, "Help me!" Our tiny terror still would not budge. My son clearly drew the battle lines, with the entire church watching.

I stepped onto the stage, heels clacking loudly on the wooden floor in the middle of a poignant song, and I physically pried my son—who was now throwing a full-on tantrum with screams and flailing limbs—off my husband, and forcibly carried him off stage in front of everyone, in the middle of (what was supposed to be) *worship*. I was overcome with embarrassment, shame, anger, and frustration. I felt like a complete and utter failure as a parent. I think a video of this incident can be found on Wikipedia next to #momfail. I will never ever forget what I felt in that moment.

We all feel like failures from time to time. Today, actually, is no exception for me. It just seems like more is going wrong than right today, and I feel like all my efforts are in vain. The truth is, I'm not failing. I'm just having a bad day. The additional truth is, if I feel like a failure, it's because I'm listening to the deceiver instead of my heavenly Father.

The enemy is quite adept at telling half-truths that we buy into wholeheartedly. With just a kernel of accuracy, the deceiver will slather layers of falsehood coated in a tempting taste of sugary half-truth, and we willingly pop that nugget of garbage in our mouth and internalize it, only to later realize we were, in fact, eating trash. Don't allow the enemy to gain a foothold in your mind. God, in contrast to the enemy, never lies, never deceives, and never misleads; He loves, forgives, and offers grace. Turn to the author of truth to discover yourself and your worth. You are not the sum of your successes and your failures! You were bought at an immeasurable price.

Let this sink in: God never gives up on us, no matter how many times we fall short.

Think of the countless verses in the New Testament that point to the failures of the disciples, Jesus's closest friends. Peter denied knowing Jesus, and Judas handed him over to be crucified for a measly amount of cash. In addition to that, I can't imagine how Jesus must have felt during His ministry, telling story after story after story to the disciples, just hoping they would finally understand the message He so desperately wanted to teach them. More often than not, the disciples didn't really "get it." In fact, they usually misunderstood His meaning altogether. Time after time, Jesus responded not with chastisement, but by trying again with a different approach. Jesus loved the disciples despite their failings, and He also loves us despite ours.

But God demonstrates his own love for us in this:
While we were still sinners, Christ died for us.
(Rom. 5:8)

We can sin, mess up, and fall short over and over, but if we turn to God and repent, we learn that no failure on our part can ever drive us to a place where Jesus's love and redemption can't reach us. When we fail, it isn't the end of the story. It is an opportunity to turn to Him and start over again, this time with wisdom and experience. He is a God of new beginnings.

No failure on our part can ever drive us to a place where Jesus's love and redemption can't reach us.

Because of the LORD's great love we are not consumed, for his compassions never fail. They are new every morning; great is your faithfulness.
(Lam. 3:22–23)

Jesus stuck with His disciples when they stumbled, and He's with us when we stumble, too. But don't just trust that God is with you when you struggle or fail. Trust that God is *within* you. The same power that turned failure into victory, hopelessness into triumph, and death into life through the resurrection story of Jesus, lives in you and me.

Do you not know that your bodies are temples of the Holy Spirit, who is in you, whom you have received from God? You are not your own; you were bought at a price. Therefore honor God with your bodies.
(1 Cor. 6:19–20)

Let me say that again. The same power that turned the failure of the cross into the victory of the resurrection lives inside *you*. I think that means, despite any failures, you are His success story.

FACING UNFAIRNESS

Life is never fair, and perhaps it is a good thing
for most of us that it is not.[3]
—Oscar Wilde

Phwack! Bounce. *Pop!* Bounce. *Phwack!* Bounce. *Pop!* Bounce.

I watch intently as the yellow-green ball zips back and forth across the hot surface of the court, willing every shot off my daughter's racquet to land perfectly placed near one corner of the baseline, then the opposite corner. It's 11–12 in a super tiebreak that's supposed to only go to 10, but someone has to win by two points. If her opponent wins this point, the match is over.

Phwack! Bounce. *Pop!* Bounce. *Phwack!* Bounce. *Pop!* Bounce.

My daughter continues to punish the ball with spin and pace, while her opponent defensively lobs it back. My sweet girl lands a forehand an inch beyond the baseline. *"Out!"* her opponent cries, and the battle ends. I watch my daughter walk to the net, shake her opponent's hand and smile, and walk to the side of the court to gather her things.

I, however, am seething with righteous anger. What my daughter doesn't realize, is that she won three different points in that tiebreaker that her opponent didn't give her credit for, by calling balls "out" that were clearly "in." The last shot was in fact out, but that was the exception. Truthfully, my daughter won that match two times over, but her opponent cheated in order to win.

My daughter walks off the court, defeated, frustrated, and holding back tears. What I want to do is vent. What I want to say is, "You beat her! You won that match when you were up 9–8 and again when you were up 10–9. Those balls were *in*! Why didn't you stick up for yourself?" But thank God, literally I thank Him, Jesus catches hold of my tongue before I can say any of it. Especially at this point in time, those words would only further inflict damage on her momentarily weak psyche.

I may not be a hot-tempered individual, but there's a whole other Mama Bear that comes out of me when you openly cheat on the tennis court, especially against my own child. How do I balance wanting my daughter to not allow herself to be taken advantage of, while still encouraging her to be the kind, generous, trusting person she already is? I don't want to change those beautiful aspects of her spirit that God has given her, but man, this is wrong, and *I am ticked right now*!

Life isn't fair. We don't need to be told this. The world has done a fabulous job of deeply entrenching this message into us through painful experiences and harsh life lessons. So why do these moments of injustice and unfairness still hurt so badly?

I will freely admit losing a tennis match ranks low on the scale of this world's wrongdoing and oppression. All manners and forms of persecution are far too common. In our current world climate, we fight the urge to gather up our families, crawl into a comfy hole, and wait for Armageddon. We fight the urge to look only to the needs and desires of those closest to us. We fight the urge to hit back when we feel we are being threatened, rather than leaning in, listening, and striving to understand the ones we feel are infringing upon us.

When life feels unfair, we often wonder:

Where is God in this mess?
Has He abandoned us?
Did we do something to deserve this?
Why did He let this happen?

Author Rick Warren in *The Purpose-Driven Life* says, "God has a purpose behind every problem."[4] Warren goes on to explain that God uses circumstances to develop our character and draw us into relationship with Him. Though He may not *ordain* every negative situation we find ourselves in (and let's face it, we often create our own messes!), our heavenly Father does *allow* them, and according to Romans 8:28–29, His aim is to bring good out of them. Frequently, that good comes in the form of a deeper connection with and understanding of God. Without hard times, we may never sense our need for a merciful, benevolent, loving God. Rest assured, His aim is always relationship and transformation; in His eyes, eternal communion with Him far outweighs our temporary discomfort.

For our light and momentary troubles are achieving
for us an eternal glory that far outweighs them all.
(2 Cor. 4:17)

When the storms rage and the waters rise, it does not mean we are abandoned. It means we have been given a perfect opportunity to turn and seek the Lord's face. Pastor Ray Altman once said that we are "heirs of God's good gifts." When bad things happen, God's goodness and generosity hasn't changed; rather, the world has changed. When we find ourselves in these "unfair" situations, try to compare the world's economy (a closed system of finite resources) with God's economy (a limitless supply of everything good). In God, our value is not determined by our circumstances, but by our very existence as His children. And as our parent, God sees a much bigger picture than we can.

Life on this earth isn't fair. It was never meant to be fair. And honestly, we shouldn't *want* it to be fair. Because injustice demands payment. If life were fair, it would be *me* tested for forty days and nights by the devil himself, not Jesus. If life were fair, it would be *me* flogged in the street, not Jesus. If life were fair, it would be *me* crucified on that cross, not Jesus. He was without sin. I sin every single, stinking day.

> **Life on this earth isn't fair. It was never meant to be fair.**

For all have sinned and fall short of the glory of God.
(Rom. 3:23)

God is playing the long game, with the end in mind, but it's hard for us to see beyond today's match-ups. Jesus, on the other hand, carries every injustice the world offers upon His own shoulders, until the final day of judgment when the scales will ultimately be brought into balance.

If we want to combat the inequality in our lives and in our world, the call to action can be simply stated: Be like

> **Go beyond what's fair, and instead be good, kind, and generous.**

Jesus. Go beyond what's fair, and instead be good, kind, and generous.

Ever heard the phrase "Grace is getting what you don't deserve, and mercy is *not* getting what you do deserve"?[5] I find it so very true. We don't deserve forgiveness, redemption, salvation, and eternity with the Holy of Holies. But because of the sacrifice of Jesus, we can have that and so much more.

Thank God, life isn't fair!

FACING SELF-SCRUTINY

I'm not scared to be seen. I make no apologies. This is me.[6]
— "This is Me" from *The Greatest Showman*

"**R**eady or not, here I come!" my best friend shouted from the stairs of her back deck. We were happy, almost-kindergarteners in the middle of a blisteringly hot, central Texas summer. We ran around the yard barefoot in our very early 1980s crop tops and jogging shorts with the wide stripe down each side. I remember feeling self-conscious and a little embarrassed by my little round belly of remaining baby fat that protruded from the space between my shorts and top. I was only five years old, and already struggling with body insecurity.

In college, surrounded by thousands of beautiful young women, I became obsessed with losing weight, unsatisfied despite weighing only 100 pounds and wearing a size zero. I flirted dangerously with a full-on eating disorder, halted only by the genuine concern and frank discussions I had with my future husband, parents, and sister. For a time period as an adult, I buried my God-given gifts of worship leadership because serving in those gifts meant being on stage in front of my church where everyone could see me and—in my mind at least—scrutinize my size and appearance.

Oh, how I have struggled with the lies I tell myself, lies like: I can't. I am not enough. Everyone is talking about me and looking at me. I'm just going to embarrass myself. I'm going to disappoint my family. I will probably stink at that. I'm too weak/tired/dumb/out of shape/fat/inexperienced to do this.

All lies. Falsehoods. From the father of deception. I lived in a hell of my own making: an existence filled with merciless self-scrutiny. Why is it so much easier to believe negative things about ourselves rather than positive ones? Why are we our own worst critics?

I think we all struggle at times with insecurity and self-scrutiny, and when we do, where do we turn to find the truth about ourselves that we so desperately need to hear? We need to face the Father of Truth.

Jesus answered, "I am the way and the truth and the life."
(John 14:6a)

When we feel ourselves mentally and emotionally spiraling into a sea of self-doubt and anxiety, we need to recall the following verse and put it into practice:

We demolish arguments and every pretension that sets itself
up against the knowledge of God, and we take captive every
thought to make it obedient to Christ.
(2 Cor. 10:5)

If your thoughts about yourself are out of line with Scripture, then capture those thoughts and hold them accountable to Christ. Listen to these words from popular artist Lauren Daigle, from her song, "You Say":

You say I am loved when I can't feel a thing
You say I am strong when I think I am weak

And you say I am held when I am falling short
And when I don't belong, oh you say I am yours[7]

This is who God our Father says we are:

- Children of the Most High God (1 John 3:1–2)
- Created by Him for good works (Eph. 2:10)
- Created in His image (Gen. 1:27, Col. 3:9–10)
- The workmanship of His hands, His beloved creation (Gen. 2:7)
- The apple of His eye (Zech. 2:8)
- His delight (Ps. 147:11)

The image of God, my heavenly Father, *delighting* in me really strikes a chord on my heartstrings. I am reminded of how I gazed upon my children when they were infants, simply breathing in their scent, marveling in their tiny perfection, *delighting* in their very existence. They had done absolutely nothing to warrant or earn such affection and admiration. Truthfully, all they did was cry and poop and wear me out. Yet, they were mine, and I adored them. God is a father, too, and He lovingly gazes upon us in the same way. We don't have to earn His affection. He delights in us just as we are, simply because we are His. Author Ruth Chou Simons of *Gracelaced* says, "His delight in us is based on His character and not ours."[8]

However, knowing God sees us this way doesn't always mean we will *feel* beloved, or that we will always think the best of ourselves. Jennifer Rothschild, in her Bible study *Me Myself and Lies*, says most of our negative and worry-related thoughts begin with *"what-if"* words.[9] For example, what if I fail? What if it hurts? What if no one likes me? Rothschild explains that meditating on God's truth begins with "what *is*" words.[10] God is my comfort. God is my creator. Jesus is capable of doing anything He wants in and through me.

It should be enough to stop here. But our generous God always goes one step further. Just when we begin to understand that our heavenly Father accepts us completely, just as we are, God says this: You're not just acceptable to me. You are chosen. I *choose* you.

> God says this: You're not just acceptable to me. You are chosen. I *choose* you.

> *In him we were also chosen, having been predestined according to the plan of him who works out everything in conformity with the purpose of his will.*
> *(Eph. 1:11)*

> *But you are a chosen people, a royal priesthood, a holy nation, God's special possession, that you may declare the praises of him who called you out of darkness into his wonderful light.*
> *(1 Pet. 2:9)*

My friends, we are not just adequate or acceptable. We are chosen. God created us specifically for an integral part of His plan that no one else can fulfill.

> *Finally, brothers, whatever is true, whatever is noble, whatever is right, whatever is pure, whatever is lovely, whatever is admirable—if anything is excellent or praiseworthy—think about such things.*
> *(Phil. 4:8)*

We can find the source of many of our negative thoughts in our own feelings, and those feelings can either strengthen and serve us, or they can control and destroy us. It's no way to live, constantly scrutinizing and criticizing ourselves. Listen only to who *God* says you are. Try looking into the face of your heavenly Father, and seeing yourself through His eyes. You just might be amazed at the beauty you find there.

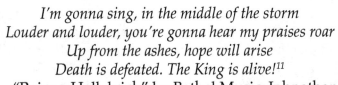

FACING DISAPPOINTMENT

I'm gonna sing, in the middle of the storm
Louder and louder, you're gonna hear my praises roar
Up from the ashes, hope will arise
Death is defeated. The King is alive![11]
— "Raise a Hallelujah" by Bethel Music, Johnathan
David Helser and Melissa Helser

An emotional dam suddenly broke open inside me. I went to the bedroom and called my husband, John, anxious and visibly shaking as I sat on the edge of the bed and said the words aloud that I was terrified to say: "I think we're supposed to adopt these babies." My husband and I had known for years that we wanted to adopt, and we had trusted God to tell us when the time was right. Suddenly, out of nowhere, that time was now.

My youngest daughter and I had spent the morning babysitting one-year-old twins. The babies were temporarily living with a friend of mine, an unofficial fostering situation through their church family. My friend had a full-time job and three children of her own, and she needed help caring for the twins that day. I was happy to help. My oldest was at school, and my youngest would love helping me "take care" of the little ones.

The entire morning was surreal. I watched myself, sitting on a blanket on my kitchen floor, spoon-feeding mac and cheese to one-year-old twins. *Twins*! I found myself so drawn to the playful, active little boy, in particular, that at one point I sat on my couch with him in my lap, clipping his fingernails and toenails. I marveled at what a maternal thing I was doing to someone else's child; yet strangely, it felt completely natural to me.

After my friend had picked the babies up, my daughter and I began cleaning the house. I stepped into her pink, purple, and aqua-colored bedroom with an armful of toys and headed to her hand-painted toy chest. I loved this room, full of joy, innocence, and imagination. My sweet girl trailed after me with her own small arms filled with toys, her light-colored pig tails bouncing. She piled the toys where I was kneeling on the floor, depositing playthings into her special bin.

And right there on the floor of my little girl's bedroom, I completely came apart. My heart broke with the knowledge that my two daughters had all these comforts and blessings, and the babies who just left our house had nothing. My stomach contracted violently. The Holy Spirit fell heavily upon me, and I knew—I suddenly and absolutely knew—we were supposed to adopt those babies.

Speaking those words aloud to my husband prompted a process of prayer, discernment, and research. John and I talked frequently with our girls about the possibility of the twins joining our family. We asked them to pray to God and ask Him to speak to their hearts about whether or not this was His will for our family. My husband made inquiries about the status of the twins and the potential for their adoption. I spoke to a few trusted friends and family members, and asked them to pray with us. After a few days, without our prompting, both of our daughter came to us, saying God was speaking to them, and they wanted us to adopt the twins. John and I felt exactly the same way.

We made our intentions known, continued to pray, and waited. Weeks later, we received a phone call from the twins' grandparents. They were so appreciative for our love and desire to adopt their grandchildren, but they had spoken with a niece and her husband, and they were also eager to adopt the twins. The babies would remain in their family, yet have a loving and healthy mom and dad.

We were so happy for this new family, yet so devastated for our own. We felt confused as to why God had directed us to pursue this course if it wasn't His will. My oldest daughter, very young and yet full of faith, asked me, "Did I hear God wrong? I don't think I did. Why did He do this to us?" We had clearly sought the Lord and acted on His leading, but nothing was happening the way we thought it would. We were completely heartbroken.

Trust in the LORD with all your heart and lean not on your own understanding; in all your ways submit to him, and he will make your paths straight.
(Prov. 3:5–6)

In our season of disappointment, we talked at length with the girls about how this outcome wasn't what we wanted, but was instead what was best for the twins. We learned that life is not always about "us" and what we want. Sometimes it's about others, and what they need. Sometimes, God tells us one thing because He wants us to act on it, but that doesn't necessarily mean everything will turn out the way we are expecting. God is smarter than us, and He sometimes puts us on a need-to-know basis. He often directs us just one single step at a time because seeing the whole picture would be more than we could handle.

Likewise, we learned that sometimes God gives us just enough information or direction to ensure we will act on it. God desires our obedience more than our understanding. He wants us to trust Him and follow Him, even when we can't see the outcome.

God desires our obedience more than our understanding.

John and I quickly realized that God used these precious twins to prompt us to start the process of becoming licensed foster parents so we could adopt. It was a time-consuming and tedious process, and if we hadn't fallen in love with the children standing before us in our home, I don't know if we would have been willing to make the sacrifices it took to become foster parents. Every minute of training and preparation was time spent away from the two children God had already given us, time forfeited for the mere hope of an adopted son who might never arrive. Additionally, we were terrified of opening a painful revolving door of foster children in our home. We didn't think our young daughters could handle falling in love with more "siblings," only to have those children leave us.

Time and prayer would teach us that we *had* heard from God, though, and we discerned His message correctly. We *were* supposed to pursue those babies, but that wasn't the end of the story. Our interest in the twins prompted their own family members to come forward to care for them, and that was God's will. Our heartbreak prompted us to start down the path that would lead us to a different baby: our son. And that was God's will for him and for our family.

But Joseph said to them, "Don't be afraid.
Am I in the place of God? You intended to harm me,
but God intended it for good to accomplish what is
now being done, the saving of many lives."
(Gen. 50:19–20)

Every bit of our "disappointment" was part of God's larger plan.

When you find yourself in your own season of disappointment, turn to your heavenly Father and pray for Him to open your eyes to what He is trying to show you and teach you. The letdown is not the end of the story; it's the turning point. Practice obedience and stand on faith, and watch with awe and gratitude as God turns your disappointment into His triumph.

FACING TRAUMA

'Cause what if your blessings come through raindrops
What if Your healing comes through tears
What if a thousand sleepless nights
are what it takes to know You're near
What if trials of this life are Your mercies in disguise[12]
—"Blessings" by Laura Story

I was leading worship at the front of the sanctuary, sandwiched between my husband to my right and my oldest daughter to my left. With an expansive view of the entire room, glass walls to the outdoors on my left, and glass doors leading to the narthex directly in front of me, I caught sight of our newly hired peace officer making her rounds through the building on this Sunday morning. In a dark flash of "what ifs," my mind imagined an instance of fear and panic during which I would catch a glimpse of *trouble* coming toward those glass doors into this sacred space of worship. I knew without so much as a conscious thought that my first move would be to turn to my left and throw myself upon my child to cover her. And I realized soon afterward that throwing myself over my beloved husband would not be an option. It's not that I don't love and adore my spouse or that I think he could not fend for himself in such a dire situation, but I know that my instinct would be to protect my child.

In this myriad of thoughts, I began to consider the love of a parent for his or her child, the kind of love that would throw itself without hesitation on an altar of sacrifice to protect the precious life of another. And I also began to consider the enormity of God's love for us because on the one hand, God is that parent, sacrificing Himself for His children through Jesus Christ. On the other hand, His love for his children en masse is so profound that instead of protecting His one Son, God sacrificed Him for all the others. How much restraint did God show to not reach down and rescue His beloved from the scourging and the crucifixion? How excruciating was it for our heavenly Father to witness the most evil and vile parts of this world heaped upon His own Son, because His every instinct is to love, protect, and care for His precious children?

I uttered a quick prayer for safety and protection over our building and all the precious souls inside, and all was well that Sunday. But others cannot say the same in other places, on other days. I struggle with prayers like this, wondering what effect they really have on a God whose will may already be in place and at work—and a God who allows bad stuff to happen to His people.

I may not have lived a very long life, but I am all too familiar with death and grief and illness and suffering, or in other words, trauma. After losing my mom, multiple other relatives, and a close friend all within a short span of time while I was still in high school, I comforted myself with the following verses:

No temptation has seized you except what is common to man. And God is faithful; he will not let you be tempted beyond

what you can bear. But when you are tempted, he will also
provide a way out so that you can stand up under it.
(1 Cor. 10:13)

And we know that in all things God works for the good
of those who love him, who have been called according to
his purpose.
(Rom. 8:28)

For now we see only a reflection as in a mirror; then
we shall see face to face. Now I know in part; then I shall
know fully, even as I am fully known.
(1 Cor. 13:12)

I reconciled in my mind, heart, and spirit that I was but a mere human, and God—in his infinite wisdom—had done the right thing by taking these loved ones to heaven when He did. I believed that somewhere, in some way that I couldn't understand, it was for the greater good; it was even for the best because God would not have allowed it otherwise.

I have since come to understand an additional truth: bad stuff happens because we live in a bad world. It's a concept called "collective sin." Because no life occurs in a vacuum, we are all affected by one another daily in a multitude of ways. Those effects can be positive or negative in nature. We may bear the effects of another's bad decisions. Someone else may bear the effects of our good ones. But our collective sin—because "all have sinned and fallen short of the glory of God" (Romans 3:23)—causes great turmoil and heartache down here on the earth. Bad things happen because people do bad things, and we all suffer for it. Justice is not guaranteed while we are here. Our very definition of "justice" is skewed by our own temporal and limited perspectives.

If we do an about-face, however, we can see that the opposite also holds true. Good things happen because people do good things. It stands to reason that the more goodness we put into the world, the better off we all become.

Do not be overcome by evil, but overcome evil with good.
(Rom. 12:21)

We can overcome evil by doing good.

We can look at the state of our world during the coronavirus pandemic to see this principle in action. Frightened people caused product shortages, for example, by selfishly buying more than they needed. On the other hand, we saw friends and neighbors offering what little they had to one another so everyone's needs could be met.

> We can overcome evil by doing good.

This world is fallen and imperfect. Traumatic situations arise daily. We don't have all the "why" answers, but we can trust the one who does. He didn't promise ease and comfort. He promises to be with us. He promises to love us no matter what. He promises to forgive us if we cling to the sacrifice and example of Jesus. And He promises that at the final trumpet call, justice will prevail, and good will finally, ultimately, eternally win.

And trauma will be forever laid to rest. Hallelujah and Amen.

FACING FEAR

I'm no longer a slave to fear. I am a child of God.[13]
—"No Longer Slaves" by Bethel Music,
Jonathan David Helser and Melissa Helser

"A*gghhh! Oh my God, Johnathan,*" my best friend screamed from the bathroom. We jumped off the living room couch and ran toward the turmoil until we heard uncontrollable laughter following the shriek. My husband and I had hosted my best friend and her husband for dinner that evening. We had put our children to bed hours before, while the adults continued to visit in hushed tones in the living room. My best friend had gotten up to go to the bathroom when we heard her screaming. Apparently as she sat on the toilet, my toddler jumped out from behind the shower curtain, yelled "Hiiiii!" at her, and nearly killed her from shock with his sneak attack. He'd sat in the tub for hours, just waiting for an opportune moment. We thought he'd been soundly asleep in his bed for hours. He laughed maniacally at the shocked adults surrounding him.

To this day, my friend can't use the bathroom in my house without first checking behind the shower curtain. Scary experiences imbed themselves in the hard-wiring of our brains and bodies. It's so hard not to be afraid.

Fear is my constant companion today. Perhaps I should be ashamed to admit that, but it's nonetheless a fact. I sit here writing this passage at my kitchen table, my laptop in front of me, a cup of hot coffee to my left, and my cell phone and Bible to my right. The morning sun is just starting to rise above my neighbor's roofline, piercing my right eye and illuminating the tall kitchen cabinets. I keep obsessively checking that dang phone. Is the ringer on? Is the volume on the ringer turned up?

I'm expecting a call from a doctor, a call that might drastically change my life. It might go something like this, "Nicki, I didn't like what I saw on those last tests. I want a biopsy." I might have breast cancer, according to the two small lumps I discovered in my left breast last week. A doctor appointment, a mammogram, and an ultrasound later, and here I am, waiting for a call.

I've spent the last forty-eight hours trying desperately to control my fear and anxiety. I've done fairly well. But the mind is a big, scary place, where you can be focused on your fourth grader's math homework while he sits in front of you snacking on pretzels, and simultaneously listening to an endless refrain of "what ifs" in your brain. Fear is a tricky business. So often it comes screeching in, sirens wailing, and surprises us, stopping us dead in our tracks before we can even grasp the reality of what is going on. God obviously knew fear was going to be particularly difficult for us humans. After all, He mentioned variations of the word *fear* more than 500 times in the Bible. The common thread for all those occurrences? "Do *not* be afraid." Humph. It seems clear to me that God knew fear would be a hard one for us to conquer.

I don't know about you, but my mind will betray me every time, leading me down an anxiety-riddled path of worst-case scenarios. My mother died of liver cancer when I was barely fifteen years old. I don't have a false sense of security when it comes to cancer; her death shattered that. Bad things do happen. People do get cancer. The most important person in your world can die, and sometimes they do. Sometimes fear is based in the unknown, but all too often, it's based in experience.

Pastor Craig Groeschel says, "God showed me that what I feared the most revealed where I trusted God the least."[14] How do we conquer our deepest fears, and develop trust in God in these areas of our lives?

I know I can't listen to *myself* when fear is crouching at my door like a lion. I have to silence my own voice and listen to the voice of my heavenly Father. I have to intentionally seek out and meditate on the word of God. On truth. On His promises. And no, He doesn't say "Oh, it will all be all right. It's all going to turn out like you want," because He's not a magic, wish-granting genie. He's the God of the entire universe. His ways are higher than ours. His agenda is beyond our comprehension. His love is unfathomable. And, His will is always for the good of those who love Him (Rom. 8:28).

Peace I leave with you; my peace I give you. I do not give to you as the world gives. Do not let your hearts be troubled and do not be afraid.
(John 14:27)

Filling my mind with His Word reminds me of His ways and His love, and it results in peace—a peace that defies understanding. The situation may not be okay, but

I myself will be okay. Because I reside in the arms of my heavenly Father.

In the meantime? I will try not to look too far ahead. Instead, I will focus on being truly present in the current moment. When I feel my mind spinning out of control and my breath quickening, I literally practice the meditative 4-7-8 breathing technique to calm down and re-center myself. I will just keep putting one foot in front of the other, going about my day and trusting that God is directing and correcting my overall course.

When I am afraid, I put my trust in you. In God,
whose word I praise—in God I trust and am not afraid.
What can mere mortals do to me?
(Ps. 56:3–4)

Pastor Ray Altman once stated in a sermon, "God doesn't ask us to do anything unless He intends to abundantly bless us and others through it." The tricky part is knowing which things God is asking us to do, and which things this sinful world is throwing in our faces like Molotov cocktails. But know that if we are frozen with doubt and immobilized by fear, God can't bless us. If we want to catch blessings, we have to have open hands, not closed fists.

There is no fear in love. But perfect love drives out fear,
because fear has to do with punishment. The one who fears is
not made perfect in love.
(1 John 4:18)

I'm still waiting on my phone call. Am I afraid? Yes, a little bit. Thank God, literally, I'm not sitting here alone, though. Jesus is sitting right beside me. I may not know what the future holds, but I know who holds my future, and His love for me is perfect.

Facing Terror

I will not fear the terror of night nor
the arrow that flies by the day.
Though ten-thousand may fall, it will not come near
He'll guard us in all our ways.[15]
—"Psalm 91" by Mark Swayze Band

Global pandemic. War. Natural disasters. Military and civilian coups. Genocide. Terrorism. Decline of Christianity. What in the name of all that is holy is happening in our world, God?

I have a friend from high school, who spent many years as a missionary in the Middle East with her husband and young children. I prayed for their safety and their mission to spread the Gospel. I greatly admired their sacrifice and dedication. Even so, I worried they would be sitting in a café with their children when a car bomb or suicide bomber would detonate. During moments of ignorance and weakness that I am ashamed to admit, I questioned her choice to raise her children in such a dangerous environment. Today, I realize parents in other parts of the world must wonder why we Americans choose to raise *our* children *here*, in a society where mass shootings have become the norm. It seems no corner of the world is safe from terror.

Author Brené Brown discusses terrorism and its effects, saying, "Terrorism is time-released fear. Its ultimate goal is to embed fear so deeply in the heart of a community that fear becomes a way of life. This unconscious way of living then fuels so much anger and blame that people start to turn on one another ... Then it's only a matter of time before we become fractured, isolated, and driven by our perceptions of scarcity."[16]

The same rule applies to so-called "natural" terror in our society. Everywhere in America, grocery store patrons ransack shelves in advance of bad weather. A respiratory virus caused a national toilet paper shortage, of all things. We often react to terror and perceived threats of terror with selfishness. Let's face it: we don't typically behave well when we feel threatened. This is why it's illegal to yell "fire" in a crowded building, because we will trample each other to death trying to save ourselves first.

Insecurity breeds fear, and fear deceives. Fear also divides, conquers, and kills.

I think it's human nature to wonder where God is when everything appears scary, dark, and tragic. We can blame the prince of darkness, and yes, ultimately it is his fault. But responsibility proves itself a little less simple than that. We are *all* responsible. When sin first entered the world through Adam and Eve, humankind fell out of intimacy, communion, and right-standing with God. Sin separated us from Him. That's why we need Jesus, to bridge that gap and atone for our lack of holiness in the presence of a perfect God. The world we live in is horribly broken. Sin begets sin begets, you guessed it, more sin. And we all feel the effects of it, indeed, the consequences of it. We are responsible for our communal pain and suffering.

Have you ever watched a child make a bad decision, knowing that things would not end well after his choice? In those cases, discipline isn't even necessary. Life takes care of it. The child will experience the natural consequences of his choice. Hopefully the child learns to make a better choice the next time he is presented with a similar situation.

I think God looks at us this way. He's watching. He knows. He allows us to experience the result of our free-will decision-making. He feels for us. He helps us. And He hopes next time His children will make a better choice. The tricky part is that we live in a community. So even if our decision-making is good, someone else's may not be, and we may feel the effects of their choices. Why? Because God loves that person too. He loves us all. He gives us all the same free will, the same do-overs, and the same chance after chance after chance to make a better choice next time. And praise Him that He does, because He and I both know that I myself tend to make the same mistakes over and over again. We—the collective world of we—are our own worst enemies. We are all capable of both horrible and beautiful things.

The writer of Lamentations expresses our terror and anguish well, and eventually our faith and hope:

I remember my affliction and my wandering, the bitterness and the gall. I well remember them, and my soul is downcast within me. Yet this I call to mind and therefore I have hope: Because of the LORD's great love we are not consumed, for his compassions never fail. They are new every morning; great is your faithfulness. I say to myself, "The LORD is my portion; therefore I will wait for him."
(Lam. 3:19–24)

There is still much more goodness in this world than evil. When nightmares turn into reality and terror shows up at your door, ask God for eyes to see His goodness at work in the world. The battle is fought first in our minds, where the enemy slips in his little lies until they become ingrained in our thinking. Often, we don't recognize these thoughts are not our own.

Since, then, you have been raised with Christ, set your hearts on things above, where Christ is, seated at the right hand of God. Set your minds on things above, not on earthly things. For you died, and your life is now hidden with Christ in God.
(Col. 3:1–3)

> When nightmares turn into reality and terror shows up at your door, ask God for eyes to see His goodness at work in the world.

Don't be a tool in the hands of the enemy, spreading hate and fear and discord. Resist the urge to look to your own needs first. In the midst of terror, seek the good. Be the good. Trust in God's faithfulness, His provision, and His plan.

Mister Rogers loved to tell others, "When I was a boy and I would see scary things in the news, my mother would say to me, 'Look for the helpers. You will always find people who are helping.'"[17] In the midst of terror, remember to look for the helpers—the ones acting out of love. Remember to choose love. Always, always love.

FACING SIN

Are you hurting and broken within?
Overwhelmed by the weight of your sin?
Jesus is calling.
Have you come to the end of yourself?
Do you thirst for a drink from the well?
Jesus is calling.[18]
—"O Come to the Altar" by Elevation Worship

I looked out the kitchen window and could see my little boy in the backyard on his hands and knees, wearing cowboy boots, denim shorts, a long sleeve shirt, and a baseball cap—none of which matched. He was digging in the dirt and pouring soil one scoop at a time from one place to another, scattering it all over himself in the process. From yards away, I could see the dirt and mud smeared across his face and clothes. Sticks, rocks, and dirt—what more could a little boy want?

I dried my hands with a kitchen towel and went to the back door, hollering out a five-minute warning before he'd need to come inside. I'd already put supper in the oven, and there was just enough time for a bath before the family would all sit down to eat. I mentally geared up for the impending battle. You'd think I was about to ask a vampire to crawl into a boiling bath of garlic-filled holy water for all the protest I knew he'd mount. Boy, was I right. "I'm not dirty!" he countered. "I don't want a bath!" he whined. "I'm not getting in the tub!" he argued. But I'm the mom, and I know better. I had watched him play and make a mess outside. I know he needs a bath. He's filthy and covered in dirt. He may be comfortable in his current situation, but I know how much better he will feel once he's clean.

Despite his objections, I helped him bathe. And just like the night before and the night before that, he leaped from the bathtub completely naked, allowed me two seconds of towel drying, and quickly streaked through the entire house screaming, "Naked boy! Naked boy! Here comes the naked boy!" He squealed with laughter at his big sisters' horror, just like every night, and relished every second of Mom and Dad pretending to chase him. It's his favorite time of day, and yet he fights it every single time.

When it comes to sin, we are just like my son. We are God's toddlers, stewing in our own filth, trying to convince ourselves and our Father we don't need a bath. Truthfully, we know we're dirty. God knows we're dirty. And we know that God knows that we're dirty. Yet just like Adam and Eve hiding in the garden of Eden after they ate that forbidden fruit, we still try to hide our mess from our Maker.

Genesis 2 recounts the familiar fall from grace for the earth's first man and woman. The serpent tempted Eve, and she caved. Then Eve becomes the tempter, and Adam caved. After they sinned, the couple realized they were naked, so they made coverings for their bodies. Next, they "heard the sound of the Lord God as he was walking in the garden in the cool of the day, and they hid from the Lord God among the trees of the garden" (Gen. 3:8).

Finally, God called out to them, desiring to spend time with his beloved children.

First, temptation. Second, sin. Third, shame and concealment. Fourth, hiding. Fifth, loss of intimacy and fellowship with God.

When I read the creation story, I am always amazed at just how quickly Adam and Eve went from paradise-on-earth to shame and hiding from God, or paradise lost. Unconfessed sin festers and breeds additional temptation to sin in even more ways, blocking communion with our heavenly Father. All God wants to do is help us get clean so we can enter into His perfectly spotless, holy presence, and spend time with Him. But like the spiritual toddlers we are, we fool ourselves into thinking we can somehow conceal our sinfulness and dirtiness. We cannot hide from God, and trying to do so just creates an agonizing distance between us. It's just like me wanting my filthy son to get clean so he can come to the supper table and enjoy a meal with his family.

Sin is a nasty business, y'all. It literally separates us from God because God and sin cannot coexist. Anytime we put self before God, that is sin. When our actions reflect our own wants and desires instead of God's, that is sin. When we act on selfish motives instead of selfless ones, that is sin. When we choose temporary pleasure over eternal satisfaction, that is sin. When we elevate ourselves above God, that is sin. And sin always leads to suffering.

Quite often, sin looks like something we've done or a choice we've made, but sometimes it looks like something we *haven't* done.

> *If anyone, then, knows the good they ought*
> *to do and doesn't do it, it is sin for them.*
> (James 4:17)

When the Holy Spirit pricks our hearts and prompts us to do something but we do nothing, that is sin. When we know about the spiritual gifts He has placed inside us, but we allow those gifts to lie dormant while we chase our own dreams, that is sin. When we know we've been saved by the sacrifice of Jesus Christ, but we fail to tell others the Good News, that is sin.

Although God does not call us to live perfect lives, He does call us to live by the example of Christ. We fool ourselves when we claim, "I am saved! I can behave however I please because my salvation is secure!" All we are doing is cheapening the grace and mercy God offers us. That same grace and mercy cost God His only son. That same grace and mercy cost Jesus Christ His life. Forgiveness of our sins did not come cheaply.

> We fool ourselves when we claim, "I am saved! I can behave however I please because my salvation is secure!" All we are doing is cheapening the grace and mercy God offers us.

How much more severely do you think someone deserves to be punished who has trampled the Son of God underfoot, who has treated as an unholy thing the blood of the covenant that sanctified them, and who has insulted the Spirit of grace?
(Heb. 10:29)

God sees all. He knows all. And if we bring our sin into the light and confess it, He forgives all.

*Submit yourselves, then, to God. Resist the devil, and he will
flee from you. Come near to God and he will come near to
you. Wash your hands, you sinners, and purify your hearts,
you double-minded.*
(James 4:7–8)

Oh, how marvelous it feels to approach the throne of
His grace and be made clean! It's like a toddler, straight
from a smelly-good bubble bath, streaking through the
living room with a complete sense of joy and freedom,
running toward the supper table where his family
is waiting.

Nip sin in the bud early. Go to God. Confess it. Accept
the gift of atonement for your sins in Jesus Christ. Start
anew. Do better. And ease your suffering. Then, feast at
the banquet table He has prepared for us all.

FACING OBSTACLES

Satan won't bother tackling you unless you have the ball.
—Coach JuJu Scott

My day has gone completely off the rails. Some days, absolutely everything seems to go wrong. Today is a day just like that. So I enter a little diner in the heart of the Texas Hill Country, grasp a cool metal chair, and shudder as it screeches loudly as I slide it out from under the table. I sit down to a plastic tablecloth, silverware wrapped in a paper napkin, a sticky menu with a clear protective covering, and the scent of buttery homemade biscuits and sweet mesquite barbecue wafting through the air. Christian praise music fills my ears, and the daughter and elderly father at the table next to me join hands and utter a prayer before taking their first bite of food. The patrons at another table, and I swear I'm not making this up, are loudly debating whether or not "real" Texas chili contains beans.

It feels a little like home in here, and I realize I've never ventured inside the doors with my laptop in tow before; in fact, I may be the first person to ever do so. This eating establishment throws back to a slower, quieter time before we all became obsessed with the latest, greatest, fastest technology.

I sit here, writing this chapter of this book because I refuse to let the unexpected annoyances of my day keep me from this important task. A flat tire on one car, a second car that won't start, a child with a violent stomach virus, a trip to the vet, a poor doctor's report for me that recommended surgery—that's just a few of the hits that keep coming, folks. I call this a season of struggle. And dang if it doesn't always arrive when I know I am running headfirst toward a calling God has placed on me.

Obedience isn't easy, especially when the enemy is throwing up obstacles to distract and discourage us.

I've landed in the season of struggle quite a few times before. In an odd way, I find it comforting now, like a reassurance that I am, in fact, on the right track. For me, the cycle starts with disbelief about a task God has given me, then a tiny step of faith and obedience toward what He's asking, followed by nervous excitement, then pure joy as I go about the work—all while knowing I am in the heart of His will for me. About the time I hit my stride, the sky begins to fall one piece after the next, as events I can't even fathom threaten to keep me from the task at hand. It reminds me of foot-chase scenes in movies where the runner in front starts throwing trashcans and shoving shopping carts and boxes and everything they can grasp at the chaser, forcing the chaser to encounter one obstacle after another.

> *We are hard pressed on every side, but not crushed;*
> *perplexed, but not in despair; persecuted, but not abandoned;*
> *struck down, but not destroyed.*
> *(2 Cor. 4:8–9)*

When we find ourselves surrounded by obstacles, rest assured God has also surrounded us with blessings.

When we find ourselves surrounded by obstacles, rest assured God has also surrounded us with blessings.

In the midst of my trial-laden book writing, God has seen fit to bless me in an entirely different area of my life. As a worship leader, I need full use of my ears and my voice, but some medical issues (obstacles) have prevented this of late. Furthermore, due to my incredibly one-track-minded brain, the ability to sing while playing keys has always alluded me. So last Sunday, when our worship leader asked me to fill in on keys and also vocals, I came up with a long mental list of reasons why that wouldn't be possible. My mouth, on the other hand, said "Sure!"

Ummmm, Mouth, what was that you just said? I guess I figured I would just do my best and let God handle the rest. A small, imperfect offering was better than no offering at all, right? Worst case scenario, I just wouldn't sing, so I could keep the keys on tempo with the rest of the band. I remember praying with the team before worship started. I felt at peace, offered all I had to God, and asked Him to simply send His Spirit out through me.

Amazingly, I sang while playing keys that morning. And more importantly, I worshiped. And it was glorious and fun. Don't get me wrong. Musically speaking, it was far from perfect. But it was an offering of worship. I realized during that morning's rehearsal that God was not only answering my prayer to help me through my current, temporary disabilities, but He was going a step further and giving me the desires of my heart that I had never even had the courage to utter! God answered a prayer I had never even prayed: to praise Him with my voice while playing an instrument with my hands. He is so, so sweet in the ways He chooses to bless us.

> *But as for you, be strong and do not give up,*
> *for your work will be rewarded.*
> (2 Chron. 15:7)

One blessing-from-struggle we can always count on is greater intimacy with Jesus. We often ask to know God better, but what if difficult times are the means to that end? Our greatest spiritual growth occurs not in times of abundance, but in times of desperation. If anyone knew this, it was Jesus. Betrayed, beaten, mocked, and crucified, He suffered under the weight of it all. We know He physically, emotionally, and mentally felt the toll because the Bible says His sweat "was like drops of blood falling to the ground" (Luke 22:44) as He prayed at the Mount of Olives. Luke 22:42 tells us Jesus pleaded for God to "let the cup pass" from Him, but He concluded His prayer with the words "not my will but thine." Jesus modeled complete obedience to God's will, despite the pain He knew He'd endure.

Jesus knows tribulation well, and He has vowed to be with us through every step of our own. During floods, we see rainbows; after the death of a loved one, we receive affirmation of how that person impacted others' lives; during illness, we receive words and gifts of comfort from friends and family. All of this goodness comes from the source of all good: God Himself.

> *But those who suffer he delivers in their suffering;*
> *he speaks to them in their affliction.*
> (Job 36:15)

We may endure seasons of obstacles and even suffering, but God blesses us and remains beside us through it all. Our job is to look for His blessings, draw nearer to Him in prayer and study, and keep our face turned toward Him and the work He has prepared for us.

Let your eyes look straight ahead; fix your gaze directly before you. Give careful thought to the paths for your feet and be steadfast in all your ways.
(Prov. 4:25–26)

Like the runner falling behind in a chase scene as he or she encounters one obstacle after the next, we must keep our eyes fixed on the one before us: Jesus.

My meal just arrived here at the diner. It's a *huge* plate of food complete with a gigantic, brisket-filled omelet, a mountain of shredded hash browns, and two homemade biscuits. I would never be sitting here enjoying this if I hadn't unexpectedly found myself waiting on a flat tire repair this morning. Like the family at the table next to me, I choose to bow my head and pray before I take my first bite of this delicious food. I choose to thank God for this small blessing in the midst of today's crazy obstacles.

Perseverance

*Not only so, but we also glory in our sufferings,
because we know that suffering produces perseverance*
(Rom. 5:3)

FACING PERSEVERANCE

*Consider it pure joy, my brothers and sisters,
whenever you face trials of many kinds, because you know
that the testing of your faith produces perseverance. Let
perseverance finish its work so that you may be mature and
complete, not lacking anything.*
(James 1:2–4)

P erseverance is not only about trusting God, but also trusting in His ways, His methods, and His timing. It's easy to trust an all-knowing, all-present God when everything is going well, but when we find ourselves suffering long-term or wandering our proverbial desert for forty years, it's difficult to trust that God is still working in our lives. It's challenging to mentally, emotionally, and spiritually agree with His methods when it just takes *so long* to reach our "Promised Land."

How do we get to a place where we believe in both the ultimate good ending He has planned for us, and also in the everyday, little steps along the way? The answer is to seek His presence daily, to press into His Word, and to offer Him praise. We must continuously ask God to reveal more of Himself to us.

My friend, Spencer Thomas, once prayed, "God, I'm only as close to you as I want to be. Help me see the potential for my relationship with You." When we are struggling, we easily perceive barriers between ourselves and God, but they are just that: perceptions. Jesus Christ has already bridged that great divide for us.

For through him we both have access
to the Father by one Spirit.
(Eph. 2:18)

For there is one God and one mediator
between God and mankind, the man Christ Jesus.
(1 Tim. 2:5)

Jesus has also bridged another great gap on our behalf: the gap between the people we actually are, and the people God wants us to be.

Maybe we feel trapped in our circumstances or stuck in a pattern because we haven't yet learned the lessons God is trying to teach us. Sometimes, it's less about the road ahead not being prepared for us, and more about us not being prepared for the road ahead. During such times, it's easy to wonder if our suffering is all in vain. But feelings of failure, fear, doubt, and a desire to control our surroundings all run counter to our belief in a good and perfect God. If we believe He's perfect, then we don't need to fear He's making a mistake in our lives, whether it be our circumstances or His timing. When we get impatient with God, we are admitting a lack of trust. Only an intimate relationship with Him can lead us to a complete faith that perseveres.

This in-between time, between suffering and character development, strengthens our endurance and our maturity. His gifts to us during this process are His presence and His peace.

What we have received is not the spirit of the world,
but the Spirit who is from God, so that we may understand
what God has freely given us.
(1 Cor. 2:12)

You will keep in perfect peace those whose
minds are steadfast, because they trust in you.
(Isa. 26:3)

We are not alone, and we are not abandoned. Trust in the one who holds not just our future, but our present as well.

Dear God,
Thank you for being constantly good and never-changing. We can count on You, and we want You to count on us. Help us to see the possibilities and depth of a more intimate relationship with you. Help us to grow and mature, and to weather both the little things and the big things this life offers. May we bask in Your grace and mercy while we turn to You and ask for strength to persevere.
Amen.

Additional verses about perseverance:
Hebrews 12:1–3
Romans 12:12
Colossians 1:11–12
James 1:12
Hebrews 6:11
Luke 21:19

FACING EVERYDAY LIFE

The road goes on forever and the party never ends.[19]
—"The Road Goes on Forever" by Robert Earl Keen

I think fellow Kerrville native Robert Earl Keen could rewrite the lyrics to his famous song today to read "the road goes on forever and the party never starts." As I write this chapter in the middle of the coronavirus pandemic and resulting quarantine, I am longing right about now for a big (albeit safe) gathering of friends in an outdoor amphitheater, singing songs at the top of our lungs with him. But who am I kidding? I'd be thrilled to sit in a small restaurant with a handful of strangers at this point.

It baffles me how we tend to always want what we can't have. A year ago, the thought of a couple of weeks at home with no outside obligations or commitments would have sounded like a dream-come-true. Reality hits a little differently, though, when it is thrust upon us with no warning and no other options.

When everyday life at home becomes all that life has to offer, where do we turn for fulfillment and joy? No matter the season of life we find ourselves in, we dream of more exciting times and events; but, what do we do with the days we've been given? What does God expect from us *in the meantime* or, in other words, in our common everyday lives? Because, let's face it, everyday life can feel somewhat pointless and unending. Oftentimes, when we experience this sense of drudgery, it comes as the result of our comfort, not our discomfort like we may initially think.

Evangelist, author, and speaker Christine Caine says, "Settling for what is comfortable is one of the biggest enemies of our enlargement."[20] So, if we're not growing, we're stagnant. And stagnation leads to premature death—death of our dreams, our spiritual lives, and our callings.

When facing the monotony of daily life, how do we tap into a supernatural, miraculous God? Where do we find motivation to love deeply, create imaginatively, and serve joyfully? The answer lies in the acknowledgment of whom we serve as we go about each typical day.

And whatever you do, whether in word or deed,
do it all in the name of the Lord Jesus, giving thanks
to God the Father through him.
(Col. 3:17)

I don't think this verse ever pierced my heart the way it did during the pandemic quarantine. While we were literally confined to our homes and the members of our nuclear families, each day began to feel like the former, and tomorrow already looked like today. Variety was hard to come by in confinement. Yet, God continued to reveal Himself in both familiar and new ways, if I bothered to look. I saw Him in the smiles of my children, in the heart-shaped messages of ordinary objects He left in my path, in the news of kindness in my community, in the greetings and waves of normally silent or formerly preoccupied neighbors up and down my street, and in the millions of people that sought worship online.

God was and is very present and active, even when we feel bored of our routines. Jesus himself confirmed this, saying:

> *My Father is always at his work to*
> *this very day, and I too am working.*
> (John 5:17)

In both the seen and the unseen, we can trust that God is busy, working "for the good of those who love him, who have been called according to his purpose" (Rom. 8:28). In light of this, we can trust that although the visible lives before us may seem dull or stuck in neutral, we have a God behind the scenes, weaving together a beautiful tapestry of grace and redemption. And with this trust, we can turn our own labors, both easy and difficult, into works of celebration and praise. Faithfulness in our everyday tasks is an act of worship, friends!

When we shift our focus to our true provider, we experience gratitude for the things we might otherwise take for granted.

> *Don't be deceived, my dear brothers and sisters.*
> *Every good and perfect gift is from above, coming down*
> *from the Father of the heavenly lights, who does not change*
> *like shifting shadows.*
> (James 1:16–17)

This gratitude is key to understanding that God cares more about our journey than He does our destination. He cares more that we walk alongside Him than He desires for us to run ahead of Him and grab hold of first place. He cares more about our progress than our perfection. Endurance is the very stuff of ordinary days, as is perseverance.

*Therefore, since we are surrounded by such a great cloud
of witnesses, let us throw off everything that hinders
and the sin that so easily entangles. And let us run with
perseverance the race marked out for us, fixing our eyes on
Jesus, the pioneer and perfecter of faith. For the joy set before
him he endured the cross, scorning its shame, and sat down
at the right hand of the throne of God. Consider him who
endured such opposition from sinners, so that you will not
grow weary and lose heart.*
(Heb. 12:1–3)

Notice how the Scripture says we are to fix our eyes
on Jesus, not the obstacles or hindrances or sin in front
of us. Furthermore, it was "the joy set before him" that
helped Jesus endure the cross. We, too, can look to our
future in order to endure the present—to not "grow weary
and lose heart." If Jesus could look to future joy, knowing
he was about to endure the crucifixion, we can certainly
endure the inconveniences in our own lives while looking
forward to an eternity with Him.

Set your minds on things above, not on earthly things.
(Col. 3:2)

With our gaze set on our Savior, the momentary troubles of the here and now begin to soften, and the drudgery of a common day begins to hold joy. It all depends on where we look. We can face the day, or we can face the Creator of the day.

We can face the day, or we can face the Creator of the day.

He is before all things, and in him all things hold together.
(Col. 1:17)

May you see Him when you look for Him, and may you find Him where you seek Him. Start each day with the Lord. The road may feel like it goes on forever, but remember, there's an eternal party at the end.

FACING WEAKNESS

*God is more likely to give you a ministry out of your
weakness than out of your strength.*
—Rev. Howard Huhn

A scene in the car with a five-year-old:
Child: I ... can't ... get ... them ... on! Ugh!!
Me: What is going on back there?
Child: These shoes *hate* me!
Me: Sweetie, shoes don't have feelings.
Child: Well, this *left one* does!

The struggle is real, as we like to say in the Carlson
household. My son may have been struggling to get
his shoes on, but the deeper struggle he faced was with
his own weakness. Like many of us, he chose to blame
the object he was doing battle with, rather than himself.

We all face secret and not-so-secret battles. I have
struggled for as long as I can remember with a secret
weakness: my relationship with food. Dang. It hurts
writing that, and it hurts even more knowing all of you
are reading it. I am ashamed. When I was in college, I
flirted dangerously with anorexia. Truth be told, I was,
in fact, anorexic; I was just incredibly blessed to have a
boyfriend and family members who intervened before I

did serious damage to myself. In the years since then, my weight has been a complete yo-yo. I diet. I gain. I exercise. I don't exercise. I fast. I eat. I get excited when I'm losing. I hate myself when I'm heavy. I hate myself when I'm light. I get motivated. I lose motivation. And the cycle just continues.

Lose. Gain. Lose. Gain. Repeat ad nauseum. The only constant was my hatred for my body. In the midst of my circular trajectory, I comforted myself with the words of well-meaning loved ones:

- "If coffee/diet soda is your only addiction, I think you're fine!"
- "Relax! We're celebrating. Have a piece of cake. Have two!"
- "If that's your only vice, you have nothing to complain about."
- "Are you *still* doing that (fill in the blank) diet?! I tried that and it didn't work for me."
- "You eat like a bird. I could *never* eat like that."
- "You don't need to diet. You eat so healthy!"

I convinced myself that my preoccupation with food was a "lesser sin." Yet I still felt shame and failure because of it. Our society tends to shame fat people while completely accepting and even encouraging the behaviors that lead to obesity. It's a double-edged sword.

I speak constantly about the importance of balance in life, yet when it comes to food, I can never seem to find it. The fallout? Terrible self-image and hatred of my own body, both of which interfere with ministry opportunities that put me in front of others, including my own daughters. The last thing I want is to pass this body-hatred on to them, the way my mother and grandmother modeled it to me.

Instead of making excuses for my struggles, today I am confronting the lies I have believed for as long as I can remember: Food is a comfort. Food equates to fellowship and connection. Food is a reward. I know this is all incorrect. Food is sustenance and little more; it is a means-to-an-end of keeping our bodies alive. I do believe God created food partially for our enjoyment (He did declare it all "good"), and Jesus frequently chose to minister and teach over the course of fellowship surrounding a meal. However, any overindulgence of a good thing equates to sin, and anything that preoccupies our minds that is not God-centered is also sin. Food itself is not the enemy, but neither is it my friend.

I pray that confronting these fallacies will be freeing and that I will change. Somewhere deep inside I know that even if that's true, I will still struggle. I'm not pretending to have the answers or have it all together. I'm simply hoping that my story, my ministry of struggle, will resonate with someone and somehow help. No struggle means no testimony. When we don't struggle, we don't testify. It is through our weakness that God reveals our great need for Him, which allows His power to manifest in and through us.

Author and Pastor Craig Roeschel says, "God can do more through your surrender than you can with your control."[21] I want to surrender this part of my life to Jesus. I want to embrace myself fully, not the ideal mental version of myself that I can never obtain, and not just the "me" I once was or that I envision I someday will be again. I am here now, and "now" is a gift He has given me to use for His glory.

But he said to me, "My grace is sufficient for you, for my power is made perfect in weakness." Therefore I will boast all the more gladly about my weaknesses, so that Christ's power

may rest on me. That is why, for Christ's sake, I delight in
weaknesses, in insults, in hardships, in persecutions, in
difficulties. For when I am weak, then I am strong.
(2 Cor. 12:9–10)

What I perceive as weakness, God sees as potential for His greatest victory through me.

I am a work in progress, and I thank God that He's not finished with me yet. I'm very slowly learning to love this part of my nature because I know He doesn't make mistakes. My struggles are His victories. My weakness is His strength. My past has brought me to my present, and my future is in His hands. I don't want to waste a single part of what God has instilled inside of me. What I perceive as weakness, God sees as potential for His greatest victory through me.

What is your greatest weakness? What is that part of yourself that you hope no one ever discovers? Whatever it is, pray for God to show you His plans for turning it into your greatest testimony and strength. Then, trust in those plans.

Personally, I'm learning to stop chasing perfection in this area of my life. When I strive for perfection in my diet, I inevitably fail, beat myself up for failing, and then give up. I'm an all-in kind of girl. So instead of "perfect," I'm striving to choose "better," and to be content with that.

God doesn't expect our perfection. He expects our best efforts as we rely on Him for strength. He expects our devotion to Him. He expects our whole hearts. Believe it or not, He expects to pick us up when we inevitably fall and fail. He expects us to get up and try again, and to ask for His help. He expects us to turn to Him in our weakness, and allow His strength to carry us.

> *If I must boast, I will boast of the*
> *things that show my weakness.*
> *(2 Cor. 11:30)*

I don't know if you're facing an epic battle of addiction or depression, or if your battle is more shoe-string proportions like my son, but the Lord promises He is with you in the midst of it all. In your weakness, turn to Him and find strength, then go and testify to what the Lord has done.

FACING CHANGE

Change is the law of life, and those who look only to the past or the present are certain to miss the future.[22]
—John F. Kennedy

Sitting at my kitchen table, I glance outside in the morning light and notice the peach tree the kids and I planted is going through some changes. Although Peachy, as we affectionately call her, currently shows off a brilliant spectrum of green, yellow, orange, and brown accessories, I know these colors actually equate to loss. It's November now, and we've finally had some cool temps mixed in with our infamous Texas heat. I walk outside and watch Peachy's leaves dancing gracefully to the ground in the breeze, others already strewn beneath her like a quilt.

Autumn boasts so much beauty. My favorite season, by contrast, is spring. I love to watch Peachy pregnant with buds, promising a burst of pink flowers that will later wilt and turn into seeds hiding inside big, ripe, luscious fruit in late June and early July. I absolutely believe peaches are a direct gift from God.

Today, however, I'm struck by the beauty of Peachy letting go of the fruit-bearing season that was and preparing for the slower season that is yet to come. Maybe I am commiserating, as my firstborn is in her first year of college, and I'm watching my two younger children with an all-too-knowing sense of how quickly my season of child-rearing is coming to an end. Maybe it's because new ministries are calling for me to let go of former ones. Maybe it's because I just reached a milestone birthday. All I know for sure is that *my* leaves are turning yellow too.

There is a time for everything,
and a season for every activity under the heavens:
a time to be born and a time to die,
a time to plant and a time to uproot,
a time to kill and a time to heal,
a time to tear down and a time to build,
a time to weep and a time to laugh,
a time to mourn and a time to dance,
a time to scatter stones and a time to gather them,
a time to embrace and a time to refrain from embracing,
a time to search and a time to give up,
a time to keep and a time to throw away,
a time to tear and a time to mend,
a time to be silent and a time to speak,
a time to love and a time to hate,
a time for war and a time for peace.
(Eccles. 3:1–8)

The times, they are a-changin'. Constantly. The atmospheric seasons on this earth remind us that nothing here is permanent because everything exists in a constant state of change. Let me say that again: all life exists in a constant state of change. What an oxymoron! It's no wonder we have a hard time with this concept. For me, the "letting go" part of change proves the most difficult because I must exchange the familiar for the unfamiliar. In order to leave one season and enter another, I must leave the comfort of the past and present and forge ahead into an unknown future.

God once called His people, through Moses, to enter a new season. He told them to leave their familiar circumstances in Egypt to travel to an only-dreamed-about Promised Land. We know those "familiar circumstances" included slavery and bondage, but to venture out across the sea and a desert with an army chasing after them? It didn't sound so inviting. But God had bigger and better plans for His people. He had literally prepared a paradise "flowing with milk and honey" (Exod. 3). All He asked was that they follow Him there. He asked them to obey.

"For I know the plans I have for you," declares the LORD,
"plans to prosper you and not to harm you,
plans to give you hope and a future."
(Jer. 29:11)

There's an image floating around of a child clutching a teddy bear to her chest, while Jesus stands before her with an open hand, asking her to give it to Him. The child says, "But I love it, God," and Jesus says, "Trust me," while holding a teddy bear out of her sight that is three times larger, ready to release it to her. I don't know about you, but I am totally that child. I cling to what I have for fear of losing it, instead of trusting that God's plans are better for me. He holds a storehouse of blessings that I can't see, but I settle for what's right in front of me—all because change involves unknown factors. I laugh at my own absurdity, because the very things I am so desperate to hold onto are not really mine to begin with; they are all simply given by or on loan from the Father in the first place!

*Every good and perfect gift is from above, c
oming down from the Father of the heavenly lights,
who does not change like shifting shadows.*
(James 1:17)

Even though we live in a state of constant change, the aberrations we experience in this life do not apply to Father God. He remains steadfast. Consistent. Never changing. Always present. Our response to Him, on the other hand, waxes and wanes for all kinds of reasons—sin, lack of discipline or study, and anger, to name a few. We experience a variety of seasons in both our physical and spiritual lives. Have you ever stopped to wonder why we face these cycles?

Even though we live in a state of constant change, the aberrations we experience in this life do not apply to Father God.

I believe God uses the low times to draw us near to Him, and to awaken within us our great need for His perfect protection, direction, and comfort. When life is challenging, remain steadfast and hopeful, trusting He has cleared a path out of the present wilderness and into a Promised Land. Who's to say that the change we are dreading won't actually turn out better for us than we can imagine?

The high times serve to energize, renew, and ignite our passion for living out the callings He has placed on us—callings that require us to use His good gifts to bring others into His kingdom. When we feast on His mountaintop, we should drink in all the goodness we can and learn all we can about His character while we're there, to prepare for the inevitable difficulties and low times to come.

These highs and lows constitute the ebb and flow of life. Whatever season we find ourselves in, we can strive to maintain a kingdom-focused perspective by seeking God's face and not just His hands. Read Scripture. Fill your home and car with praise music. Recite the many names of God. Pray without ceasing.

Know that when God is calling us into a different phase or season, He may be asking us to leave behind a former one. Trust in His goodness. Follow Him and obey. And don't forget to dance like the changing leaves, for there is beauty in letting go and experiencing all of God's seasons.

FACING EMPTINESS

This world has nothing for me, and this world has everything.
All that I could want and nothing that I need.[23]
—"This World" by Caedmon's Call

S teaming cups of coffee in hand, Christmas wrapping paper and bows strewn all over the floor, the lights on the tree still glowing, and my husband acting like the biggest, happiest kid of all with his brand-new, surprise gift, top-of-the-line smartphone in his hot little hands. These days it's common to buy new phones every year or two, but in the early 2000s, this was a rare, expensive, pinnacle gift. He couldn't wait five minutes to start programming his new favorite gadget.

Our two-year-old son was fascinated and eager to understand Daddy's excitement at this novel, palm-sized gadget. So Dad carefully handed the phone to the toddler, and as soon as the cool metal hit our son's tiny hands, he chunked that phone as hard as he could onto the tile floor. *Craaaaack!*

We all stood perfectly still in utter disbelief, afraid to move or speak. My husband eventually stooped down to pick up the phone, which was lying face-down, only to discover the screen shattered into dozens of pieces. That phone was toast, and it had only been turned on for two or three minutes.

It's amazing how quickly the precious thing that has captivated our desire and attention for months—or even years—can completely let us down. And that's why storing treasure here on the earth is a pointless endeavor.

Do not store up for yourselves treasures on earth, where moths and vermin destroy, and where thieves break in and steal. But store up for yourselves treasures in heaven, where moths and vermin do not destroy, and where thieves do not break in and steal. For where your treasure is, there your heart will be also.
(Matt. 6:19–21)

We look to this world for satisfaction, but we can't find it here. Our culture is obsessed with immediate gratification. We can acquire anything we want as soon as our minds can conceive it! Phones, computers, household appliances, electronics—everything is faster, smarter, and better. They're also obsolete, broken, and outdated long before we have finished using them and needing them.

The world's offerings are temporary because this world has been in decay, atrophying, since the fall of man in the garden of Eden. Nothing here will last. All we can find are solutions with expiration dates. No wonder we feel empty!

When we fail to make God our first love—the object of our affections—we feel like we're driving around town with a rapidly draining tank of gas, sputtering and stalling and near-total death. We're constantly running on empty. That's because God didn't design us to chase a hundred different things at once. Heck, He didn't design us to chase after *anything* other than Himself. God designed us to love and praise Him. That's it! He is a jealous God who doesn't want to share our affection or attention with other anyone or anything else. Anything that diverts our focus from God is a form of idolatry. The truth is, we all worship something or someone; the question is what (or whom) we allow to be our Master.

No one can serve two masters. Either you will hate the one and love the other, or you will be devoted to the one and despise the other. You cannot serve both God and money.
(Matt. 6:24)

It is so easy to set ourselves up as our own masters. I constantly hear women admonishing each other these days with the phrase, "Girl, you can't pour from an empty cup." Although the statement is absolutely true, the solution commonly offered is "self-care." In our current culture, self-care advocates claim we have drained our emotional, physical, and mental well-being, so we need to rest, tap back into our own strength, and get back out there! This might look like a spa day, reading a romance novel, enjoying a glass of wine, opting for a date night, or going out with your girlfriends. None of these things is wrong or a poor choice, but rest assured, these activities alone are not going to refill these empty cups of ours. What happens tomorrow when we pour ourselves out on everyone and everything around us and find ourselves dying of thirst yet again?

No. The only thing—the only one—who can fill that achingly empty cup of ours, is God.

On the last and greatest day of the festival,
Jesus stood and said in a loud voice, "Let anyone who is
thirsty come to me and drink. Whoever believes in me,
as Scripture has said, rivers of living water will flow from

within them." By this he meant the Spirit, whom those who
believed in him were later to receive.
(John 7:37–39a)

We all sense the emptiness in our cups. We carry them around and beg everyone and everything—entertainment, sports, relationships, food, drugs, and a whole host of "not-God" things—to fill them up for us and get rid of the void. Every single one of these is immediately gratifying in some way, but it is also immediately consumed and then gone. When we allow Jesus to fill our cups, however, we tap into a well that will never, not *ever*, run dry. Jesus will not just fill our cups, but they will *overflow* and slosh out onto those around us in beautiful kingdom ways that we can't even imagine.

If we want lasting solutions to our emptiness, we must first seek things that are eternal.

My friend and fellow author, Elizabeth Oates, says what we desperately need is not self-care, but soul care. I agree. If we want lasting solutions to our emptiness, we must first seek things that are eternal. And the only thing that's eternal is God Almighty.

If we feel empty, the world cannot fill us. Seek the lover of your soul. Spend time with your best friend, Jesus. Read the love letters He has left for you in the Bible. Go on a coffee date with the one who knows you best and loves you just the way you are.

I don't know about you, but I want my cup forever-filled, and I want to splash a little Jesus from it on everyone I meet.

FACING PRAYER

I'm so confused.
I know I heard you loud and clear.
So I followed through.
Somehow I ended up here.
I don't wanna think.
I may never understand that my broken heart
is a part of your plan.
When I try to pray all I've got is hurt, and these four words:
Thy Will Be Done.[24]
— "Thy Will" by Hillary Scott

I sat idling in the preschool pick-up line with the air conditioning on full blast. It was another sweltering Texas day. My sweet girl bounced into the car and immediately asked, "Can we stop for ice cream?" I considered the time of day, my plans for a healthy supper, our lack of plans for the afternoon, and then offered an enthusiastic "yes" to an ice cream date with my daughter. The next day on the way home from school, my precious darling once again asked, "Can we stop for ice cream?" I considered all the same things I had the day before, this time adding in my child's sugar and fat intake, the financial cost of a daily treat, the pattern I might be establishing, and this time said "no."

Now, put yourself in the mental perspective of my four-year-old. What changed? Yesterday you were going home from school. You asked for ice cream. Mom said yes. Same thing today, only today she said no. From the child's limited understanding, nothing has changed except Mom's answer. How does the child make sense of this? Many scenarios come into play: Mom is mean. Mom is mad. Mom is punishing me. Mom doesn't like me anymore. The jig is up—Mom will never let me have ice cream again.

Now, put yourself in the parent's perspective. A great deal more information came into play on day two. I, the parent, was looking beyond the "right now" into the "not yet." And now I, the parent, whose only goal was to love and do the very best for my child, is completely misunderstood. This is how many of our prayer lives often look, my friends. We ask for something we want, and God (in His infinite knowing) decides what is best, and we (in our lack of knowing) make all kinds of assumptions based on His answers.

If you believe, you will receive whatever you ask for in prayer.
(Matt. 21:22)

Hear me when I say this: I have never prayed with more conviction, more frequency, or more belief than I did when my mother had cancer. I was fourteen—going on fifteen—years old, and I can say with my hand on a Bible that I absolutely believed without a doubt that He was going to heal her. It felt as if my entire town was praying for her. She was an incredible woman with faith that could move mountains and a spirit that could calm the fiercest storm. There was no way my God was going to let her die. She didn't deserve it. We, her family, didn't deserve it. My mom was going to be a living story of His miraculous healing.

But that didn't happen. When I was fifteen years old, my mother died. And yet, I continued to believe in God. I continued to trust God. I even continued to praise God. But for so many years, I was unable to reconcile the verse above and the following verse, in light of my own life and experiences:

You may ask me for anything in my name, and I will do it.
(John 14:14)

I have since learned a few things about prayer and the will of God. First, praying is not about wish-making. God is not our personal, big, fat, blue genie in the sky, awaiting our wishes and then springing into action.

When my son was four, he once told me he was "all out of happiness" because I wouldn't let him play with my iPad. I asked him, "Do you know that happiness comes from God? I bet if you ask Him, He will give you some." My precious boy was quiet for a while, then he suddenly piped up, saying, "I would like to meet a baby reindeer. That would give me happiness." I was dumbfounded, and said, "What are you talking about?" To which he replied, "I wasn't talking to *you*, Mom, I was talking to *God*."

As hilarious as the moment was, it made me realize the (natural) immaturity of my son's four-year-old faith. He was simply making his wishes known to God. And the truth is, there's absolutely nothing wrong with that. God *wants* us to speak to Him about all our wants and needs. He already knows them, anyway. The point, however, is to understand that just because we ask for something, that doesn't mean God will give it to us. The point is cultivating a relationship with God through prayer, not through the realization of our wants or perceived needs through prayer. God wants to have a conversation, not so the situation will change, but so *we* will change. We should pray, not until we feel God has heard us, but until we have heard God.

> God wants to have a conversation, not so the situation will change, but so *we* will change. We should pray, not until we feel God has heard us, but until we have heard God.

As for the tricky business of the will of God, I've come to believe this: God has a perfect will for us and a permissive will for us. His perfect will includes the major life events that He will ensure take place regardless of the choices we make. His permissive will includes the lesser choices that He allows us to make for ourselves. Imagine a parent letting a child choose whether or not to run in front of a speeding car. That's not going to happen, right? That's like God's perfect will because He will step in and ensure that outcome. Now think back to our ice cream scene. My daughter took what seemed like a lifetime to choose what flavor of ice cream she wanted that day on the way home from school. But I let her choose. It felt like a life-and-death decision to her, but I knew that it didn't really matter what flavor she chose, so I allowed her to make the choice. That's like His permissive will. The parent allows the child to choose because major life events aren't dependent on the choice.

So how does this factor into prayer? My personal frustration was praying for my mother's healing when His *perfect will* didn't include that. When we pray, we should pray, "Thy will be done," but know that it is also perfectly okay to pray for your heart's desires. God already knows them! That doesn't mean He will grant our every wish, though, especially if our requests don't line up with His perfect will.

As a parent, I cherish moments when my children pour out their hearts to me. "But I just wanted him to like me!" "Why won't you let me do this; I really want to!" "I'm so mad at her!" It's not that I can or will change the situation, but I want to hear and know their hearts because maybe after listening, I can speak and change their perspectives. At the very least, I can comfort them and reassure them of my love. And that's precisely what God wants from our prayer time with Him. He wants to change our outlook, not always our future.

God *always* answers prayer. Sometimes we like the answer; sometimes we don't. But like any good parent, He is always there, always listening, always guiding, always comforting, always encouraging. Talk to Him.

Facing Misunderstanding

*In the whole round of human affairs little is
so fatal to peace as misunderstanding.*[25]
—Margaret Elizabeth Sangster

"**M**om! We got to do a tuggle war at school today!"
"A tug of war?" I asked.

"Noooo—a *tuggle* war. You know, with the rope? And
the teams?!"

"Sweetie," I said, "it's called a *tug of war.*"

Clearly exasperated, he yelled, "*Mom!* That doesn't
even mean anything! That's not even a word!"

"And *tuggle war* is?" I quietly giggled to myself.

Few things can quickly elicit laughs like an epic
miscommunication. Sitcoms are famous for this type of
humor. Just imagine if all the friendly characters living
near each other in those sit-com apartment complexes
would just *talk to each other*; there would be no basis for
humor in these shows!

But in real life, communication mix-ups can be
exasperating and downright relationship-busting. I tend
to think there are few things in this life that deep, effective
communication cannot improve or even solve. Because
of this, it is the most gut-wrenching thing in the world
for me when someone misunderstands or misjudges

my intent or meaning. I've been guilty of mentally rehearsing conversations and then later replaying these conversations on repeat ad nauseam, literally until I am nauseous. Inevitably, I imagine a cathartic moment of clarity, accompanied by warm feelings as acceptance and empathy abound. In my actual life, however, this rarely occurs, and I am left trying to handle my own feelings of rejection and being misunderstood.

If anyone in this world can relate to the agony of being misunderstood, it's Jesus. God left heaven and came to the earth in human form so He could redeem all of His creation once and for eternity. Time and time again Jesus tried to drive home a message to the crowds, only to have them completely miss the meaning. During His earthly tenure, He was chased, accused, ridiculed, gossiped about, arrested, stood trial, beaten, flogged, mocked, and crucified—all for doing the holy work of teaching, redeeming, and saving.

That's enough to make my own communication mishaps look downright comical.

Jesus set his gaze firmly on God's plan and did not deter from it, regardless of the insults and accusations hurled His direction. He steadily taught the character of God in story form to anyone who would listen and by example to all who were willing to see. Christ did not allow those who refused to listen or understand distract Him from His mission. When He was misjudged, He attempted to make himself clear, and if that failed, He moved on.

If anyone will not welcome you or listen to your words, shake the dust off your feet when you leave that home or town.
(Matt. 10:14)

I've always experienced a little gut-check when reading that verse. *Wait, I just give up? I just let people believe something completely wrong about me? I just leave people wallowing in their own ignorance and quit trying to reach them?*

In a way, yes. We have to be content with doing what we can and allowing other people to respond in whatever way they wish. Our job is to communicate, love, and lead by example. The "understanding" part? That's out of our control and God's responsibility alone. And honestly, that's a hard one for me.

> Our job is to communicate, love, and lead by example. The "understanding" part? That's out of our control and God's responsibility alone.

For most of my life, I tried to control what others thought of me. I was a quintessential people-pleaser. I distinctly remember my father, in the hallway by our front door, cupping my face in both his hands and looking intently into my eyes and saying, "Nic, sweetie, I'm afraid you're going to have an ulcer before you even graduate high school." I absolutely agonized over others' perceptions of me. I needed to be perfect, not just for myself, but for everyone else also. What a burden I chose to carry!

I remember the first time I read the phrase "What other people think of me is none of my business." I've tried to locate the author of this phrase, but many different people claim it, probably because it's a universal truth. The first time I read this statement, I felt an empowering sense of freedom, like an immense pressure being lifted. Others' perceptions of me are outside of my control. I can't make everyone understand my motive or my meaning. My job is to be the "me" that God created, and how the world accepts that "me" is beyond my realm of influence. I must strive to communicate, but I cannot force understanding. I must possess pure motives, but I cannot interpret those motives on anyone else's behalf. I must share, but I cannot receive for my listeners. I must speak of God, but I cannot hear and understand the message for my listeners.

I think Jesus understood this well. He was there in the beginning, and He helped impart that beautiful part of us called free will, knowing He was yielding some control to us for our own decision-making and understanding. If Jesus instructed His disciples to move to the next town when they were misunderstood or rejected, I suppose I should, too.

Whoever welcomes you welcomes me, and
whoever welcomes me welcomes the one who sent me.
(Matt. 10:40)

When I'm feeling overwhelmed by the weight of expectations and commitments, I often tell my children, "I can only do what I can do." Sometimes that means fetching take-out for supper instead of cooking a homemade meal. Other times, that means I'm wearing a dress and my good jewelry and standing at the outdoor grill barbecuing steaks and veggies for an awesome supper. Sometimes that means my kids need to go make their own lunch for school tomorrow. And sometimes, that means all three tailor-made, to-their-particular-taste lunches (plus backpacks, sports equipment, snacks, and water bottles) are lined up by the back door ready to go for the next day at 5 p.m. the day before.

On any given day, we can only do what we can do. Our most important job is to be obedient to God, and to leave the outcomes in His hands. We can learn to simply do our best and not worry about how others perceive our efforts. I'm certain we will, at times, be entirely misunderstood. We may face a great many "tuggle" wars. But we're in good company. Jesus did, too.

FACING FAMILY

A happy family is but an earlier heaven.[26]
—George Bernard Shaw

H eart racing, thoughts spinning, I pulled the car off the interstate and into the nearest fast food restaurant parking lot. My tiny boy, still in preschool, posed a question that rocked my world. I knew this day would come, but I had no idea it would come so soon. I uttered silent prayers for God to direct my words, for the Holy Spirit to blanket our car, and for Jesus to comfort my sweet son's heart and give him understanding.

I put the car in park and turned off the ignition, then walked around to his door. Unbuckling him from his car seat, I stood very near and looked him in the eyes while holding his tiny hands. I tried to sound as calm and at ease as possible, though I felt like I might faint. The first of many conversations was already here, and I knew the first would be the hardest. I said, "What did you want to ask me, sweetie? Can you say it again?"

His little voice replied, "Mommy, did I grow in your tummy like my big sisters?"

I answered matter-of-factly, "No, Sweetie, you didn't."

"Then where did I grow?" he implored.

"You grew in your first mommy's tummy. And she gave birth to you." I searched his eyes for signs of understanding. This was so very much for my tiny guy to process. I waited for this information to sink in, and then allowed him to direct where this conversation would take us. His reply was everything I feared, not for myself, but for his little heart's sake.

"But where is she? Why isn't she taking care of me?" he tearfully asked.

This was a tough conversation in which my son's definition of "family" forcibly changed.

Family. It's a loaded word.

For some, "family" evokes feelings of warmth and safety, tradition, and belonging. For many others, it conjures negative emotions like rejection, anger, and even post-traumatic stress. For most of us, thoughts of family leave us with a confused mixture of all these feelings, plus many more.

If it's any consolation, the very first family—Adam and Eve and their sons Cain and Abel—was no better than us at doing this family thing. In fact, they were just about as dysfunctional as it gets, and they were the only four people living on the earth at the time! Their story is ripe with jealousy, selfishness, sibling rivalry, sin, and even murder. In fact, I can't think of a single perfect family in the entire Bible. Even Mary and Joseph became so busy with festivities and traveling that they didn't notice for an entire night and day that they had left their young son Jesus behind in Jerusalem!

Although God has an "ideal" for families, He also knows our families won't really look like His perfect vision. Why? Because families are made up of imperfect people bent on sin. Family is no heaven-on-earth, but it is a training ground for the kingdom of heaven, or at least that's how God *designed* families to operate. Within our family relationships, God gives us opportunities to live by Jesus's example and to love our families as He loves us. This is where transformation can happen, but it's not easy. God knew we would need a lot of help in this area.

God knew our earthly father would not be perfect, so He designed Himself as our faultless heavenly Father.

Be perfect, therefore, as your heavenly Father is perfect.
(Matt. 5:48)

Within our family relationships, God gives us opportunities to live by Jesus's example and to love our families as He loves us.

Every good and perfect gift is from above,
coming down from the Father of the heavenly lights,
who does not change like shifting shadows.
(James 1:17)

God knew we would often make a mess of marriage (the building block of family), so Scripture describes Him as our faithful bridegroom, and the church as His cherished bride.

Let us rejoice and be glad and give him glory!
For the wedding of the Lamb has come, and his bride
has made herself ready. Fine linen, bright and clean,
was given her to wear. (Fine linen stands for the
righteous acts of God's holy people.)
(Rev. 19:7–8)

You yourselves can testify that I said, "I am not the Messiah but am sent ahead of him." The bride belongs to the bridegroom. The friend who attends the bridegroom waits and listens for him, and is full of joy when he hears the bridegroom's voice. That joy is mine, and it is now complete. He must become greater; I must become less.
(John 3:28–30)

God knew we might feel abandoned or neglected by our earthly parents, so He tells us we are His adopted sons and daughters.

For he chose us in him before the creation of the world to be holy and blameless in his sight. In love he predestined us for adoption to sonship through Jesus Christ, in accordance with his pleasure and will.
(Eph. 1:4–5)

But when the set time had fully come, God sent his Son, born of a woman, born under the law, to redeem those under the law, that we might receive adoption to sonship. Because you are his sons, God sent the Spirit of his Son into our hearts, the Spirit who calls out, "Abba, Father."
Gal. 4:4–6

"I will be a Father to you, and you will be my sons and daughters," says the Lord Almighty.
(2 Cor. 6:18)

God knew we might not feel like we "belong" within our families, so He gave us membership in His household and citizenship in heaven.

Consequently, you are no longer foreigners and
strangers, but fellow citizens with God's people
and also members of his household.
(Eph. 2:19)

**God knew our families might squander our
inheritance, so He gave us eternal provision.**

Now if we are children, then we are heirs—heirs of God and
co-heirs with Christ, if indeed we share in his sufferings in
order that we may also share in his glory.
(Rom. 8:17)

**God knew we might face judgment, ridicule, and
criticism, instead of love and acceptance from our
families, so He declared us His beloved.**

Let the beloved of the LORD rest secure in him,
for he shields him all day long, and the one the LORD
loves rests between his shoulders.
(Deut. 33:12)

It was not by their sword that they won the land,
nor did their arm bring them victory;
it was your right hand, your arm, and the light
of your face, for you loved them.
(Ps. 44:3)

**What's the bottom line? Family may disappoint us,
but God never will.**

The LORD himself goes before you and will be with you;
he will never leave you nor forsake you. Do not be afraid;
do not be discouraged.
(Deut. 31:8)

My son claims his eternal father and family in Heaven, and that provides a sense of belonging and security that his first family here on the earth could not give him. He was not abandoned or unloved by his heavenly Father; in fact, father God arranged every detail of his life to give him hope and a future, just like Jeremiah 29:11 says.

Whether hearing the word "family" brings to the surface warm and fuzzy feelings, conflicted feelings, or intense feelings of dread for you, know that you are a valued member of the family of God. We are all siblings in Christ, and Daddy's got our heavenly home ready and waiting for us all. I don't know about you, but I am eager to get home for that family reunion.

FACING WORRY

Worry is like a rocking chair; it gives you something to do,
but never gets you anywhere.[27]
—Erma Bombeck

"Nicki, this is Carla, your case worker. We need you to bring Johnathan in for a DNA test to establish paternity. We have two potential fathers, and the outcome of the test will have a big impact on his case and availability for adoption."

The words came across the phone line and landed like a lead weight inside my body. I started asking questions, but my questions were met only with guesses layered in speculation. I convinced myself of the outcome we wanted on that DNA test, of the outcome that would greatly increase our chances of adopting this child. I fretted all day every day, tossed and turned every night, and anxiously waited for the date on the calendar when I would travel with the baby to a nearby city for the test. Afterward, I fretted and tossed and turned for days and nights following the test, while we waited for the results. I hoped and prayed the test would come out the way we wanted; I could have willed it into existence with my intense emotions. I lived with a perpetual knot in my stomach.

I was wrong on all accounts. The DNA test did *not* come out the way I wanted, or at least, not the way I *thought* I wanted. God had the situation completely under control, despite my thinking that I knew better. That DNA test led to one of the most overwhelming moments of grace in my entire life: the moment my son's birth father gave up his parental rights and said he wanted us to be Johnathan's parents. I will never as long as I live understand the strength and courage it took for that man to make such a sacrifice for our son, and I will never take for granted the indescribable gift he gave our family. To be entrusted with another's life is beyond words.

I wonder though, how much angst could I have avoided if I had trusted in God's will and not my own? How much easier could life have been if I had asked God to reach inside my heart and replace what I wanted with what *He* wanted, right from the start? What joy did I miss out on while I was busy pleading for my own way?

Worry is not quite as simple as a lack of faith, as some would say. I know plenty of people with tremendous faith, who still worry. Worry is a choice. We can choose to dwell on what-ifs, and we can choose to ruminate on our own preferred outcomes, but neither approach brings peace. We have to let go of the notion that we know what is best for ourselves and our loved ones, and trust that God alone does. We have to know that even our own wishes and desires can lead us to betray our best selves and best futures.

Control, fear, and doubt all run counter to our belief in a good and perfect God. If we

> If we truly believe God is perfect, then we have no reason to think He will make a mistake in our lives.

truly believe God is perfect, then we have no reason to think He will make a mistake in our lives. We have to develop trust in Him, and the best way to do that is within an intimate relationship built on consistently seeking greater knowledge of His character. He is a good, perfect, loving Father.

In Matthew, chapter 6, Jesus offers some straightforward instruction for us: Do not worry. In today's lingo, it might read: "Bruh, I got this. I got *you*. Relax."

Jesus knew all too well our temptation to worry, so He asked:

> *Can any one of you by worrying*
> *add a single hour to your life?*
> *(Matt. 6:27)*

The mind is a battlefield, and unbeknownst to many of us, the players in this fight are not solely us and God. A third contender whose voice we may not recognize, or may even mistake for our own, stands his ground there: the Enemy. Those fears that plague you? The worries that abound? The insecurities that taunt? That's the voice of the Deceiver himself.

You see, if the evil one can influence our thoughts, he knows that our thoughts turn into our beliefs, and our beliefs turn into actions and expectations of others. It all starts in our mind, and the great big, flashing, neon warning sign for this epic battle is none other than *worry*.

> *But seek first his kingdom and his righteousness, and all*
> *these things will be given to you as well. Therefore do not*
> *worry about tomorrow, for tomorrow will worry about itself.*
> *Each day has enough trouble of its own.*
> *(Matt. 6:33–34)*

We can't change our circumstances and outcomes at will. We especially can't accomplish this through the act of worrying. God, however, can do all things. He wants our circumstances and outcomes to change as a result of our knowledge, belief, and trust in Him and His ways. In other words, God changes *us,* and our responses, through our relationship with Him. Part of the beauty of that relationship rests in its eternal nature. God was with us in the past; He is with us now in the present; He is already with us in our future, waiting for us to join Him there. If the everlasting God of the universe is with us and for us, what can we possibly worry about?

> *If you say, "The LORD is my refuge,"*
> *and you make the Most High your dwelling,*
> *no harm will overtake you,*
> *no disaster will come near your tent.*
> *For he will command his angels concerning you*
> *to guard you in all your ways;*
> *they will lift you up in their hands,*
> *so that you will not strike your foot against a stone.*
> *(Ps. 91:9–12)*

My aunt Liz loves the saying, "Don't tell God how big your storm is, tell the storm how big your God is!" If we can remember that God holds our past, our present, and our future in the palm of His hands and that His plans are always and ever for our good (Rom. 8:28), then we have no cause to worry. Choose to focus on the infinite power of your heavenly Father, and trust that even your fondest dreams can't hold a candle to the plans He has for you.

FACING DOUBT

We doubt your goodness, we doubt your love
As if every promise from Your Word is not enough
All the while, You hear each desperate plea
And long that we'd have faith to believe.[28]
—"Blessings" by Laura Story

M y four-year-old ran toward the fountain in the center of the shopping mall, unable to contain his awe and excitement. "I want to *throw* something!" he exclaimed, bouncing up and down in front of the watery spectacle.

His big sister started rummaging around in her tiny, sparkly, little-girl purse and pulled out a single penny for him. "Make a wish, first!" Rachel instructed.

My boy-child clutched the penny tightly and stood still for two whole seconds, then hurled it into the depths of the fountain with all his might. The magical moment over, he turned to walk away.

Rachel asked, "Johnathan, what did you wish for?"

He replied, "A dinosaur."

That's right, folks. A dinosaur. Not a toy dinosaur, either. A real, live dinosaur. You know, the extinct kind. Apparently, he wants a pet—a pet *dinosaur*—to be exact.

All I could say was, "Way to dream big, buddy!"

The whole encounter is so indicative of my son. He sees no limits. He dreams impossible dreams. He wishes for the moon and stars—and dinosaurs. I love this about him. And I would love to have his child-like faith again, the kind of innocent faith that doesn't know the agony of disappointment. But as we age, we experience more of both the good and the bad that this world and life have to offer. And to quote Don Henley, "The more I know, the less I understand."[29] It can leave us jaded. And full of doubts.

Some of the greatest heroes in the Bible struggled with doubts. Take Moses, for example. God instructed Moses to go before Pharaoh in Egypt and demand the release of the enslaved Israelite people. Moses, however, questioned if God had chosen the right man for the job, questioned exactly what he would say, questioned God's ability to speak through him, and questioned if the Israelites would believe he was actually speaking on God's behalf. After God offered an answer for every excuse Moses put forth, Moses then cited his personal deficiencies.

Moses said to the LORD, "Pardon your servant, Lord. I have never been eloquent, neither in the past nor since you have spoken to your servant. I am slow of speech and tongue."
(Exod. 4:10)

Despite His frustrations with Moses's doubts, God had anticipated his reaction and already put a plan into action to help him. God said He had already sent for Aaron who would offer his strengths to counteract Moses's weaknesses.

Then the LORD's anger burned against Moses and he said, "What about your brother, Aaron the Levite? I know he can speak well. He is already on his way to meet you, and he will

be glad to see you. You shall speak to him and put words in his mouth; I will help both of you speak and will teach you what to do. He will speak to the people for you, and it will be as if he were your mouth and as if you were God to him."
(Exod. 4:14–16)

God saw Moses's ability, not his inability, and He made allowances for his shortcomings. God is faithful to accomplish His purposes through us, despite our doubts, if we are willing to trust and obey Him.

David provides another example. We read David's prayers in the book of Psalms and know that he is questioning if God has abandoned and forsaken him. On the run and surrounded by enemies, David pours out his heart to his Heavenly Father:

O God, why have you rejected us forever?
Why does your anger smolder against the sheep of your
pasture? ...
We are given no signs from God;
no prophets are left,
and none of us knows how long this will be ...
But God is my King from long ago;
he brings salvation on the earth ...
Do not let the oppressed retreat in disgrace;
may the poor and needy praise your name.
(Ps. 74:1, 9, 12, 21)

We witness in these passages David's transition from doubts to praise to faith. We, too, can turn our doubts into praise and faith by seeking God's face in prayer and worship. He is faithful to comfort, guide, and protect us, and we can rely on the Holy Spirit to help us as we pray.

Perhaps the most obvious example of doubting we can find in Scripture is Jesus's disciple, Thomas. The book

---

of John, chapter 20, explains that after Jesus rose from the tomb, He appeared privately to His disciples, but Thomas was not with them. When the men relayed to Thomas all that had occurred, he said he would not believe it unless he could see for himself the nail marks and put his hand into Jesus's side where the spear punctured Him. A week later, Jesus appeared to His friends again, and this time, Thomas was in attendance.

> *Then he said to Thomas, "Put your finger here;*
> *see my hands. Reach out your hand and put it into my side.*
> *Stop doubting and believe."*
> *(John 20:27)*

Thomas realized the futility of his doubts, in light of the resurrected Jesus standing before Him. Not only that, but Jesus knew exactly what Thomas needed to believe, and He immediately offered it to him.

> *Then Jesus told him, "Because you have seen me,*
> *you have believed; blessed are those who have*
> *not seen and yet have believed."*
> *(John 20:29)*

God doesn't need our faith to be doubt-free to accomplish His plans through us.

Jesus knew Thomas doubted, but He loved him anyway; furthermore, Jesus enacted a plan to rescue Thomas from the questions that plagued his faith. He can and will do the same for us.

Friends, God is not bothered by our questions. Our doubts do not rock His world. God doesn't need our faith to be doubt-free to accomplish His plans through us. In fact, God doesn't *need* us at all. He *invites* us to participate because He loves us and greatly desires to be in an intimate relationship with us.

So bring Him your doubts and your questions. Share your dreams with the Creator of the universe. It doesn't matter if your wishes are as grand as a pet dinosaur or as humble as a simple meal, God cares deeply for you. If spiritual giants like Moses, David, and Thomas were capable of doing mighty things for God in spite of their doubts, rest assured that we can too. Pour yourself out to Him in prayer and then watch as God miraculously transforms your heart and turns your doubts into faith.

FACING RELEASE

Breathe.
Let go.
And remind yourself that this very moment
is the only one you know you have for sure.[30]
—Oprah Winfrey

I walked slowly into the sun-filled backyard, the dormant grass and fallen leaves crunching under my bare feet. I quickly realized this was not going to be a picture-perfect moment because I immediately sneezed (thanks to the crippling cedar pollen) and then side-stepped a pile of dog poop. I created a makeshift pollen barrier by covering my nose and mouth with the end of my sleeve, and continued to walk slow circles in the yard.

I questioned if I was depressed. I questioned if I was just experiencing the throes of the all-too-normal-yet-still-agonizing mid-life changes in my body, mind, and life circumstances. I questioned if this was anxiety surrounding my kids. I questioned if I needed a vacation. I questioned if my post-hysterectomy hormones had run out and it was time for new ones. I questioned if my mood was the common result of the concussion I recently sustained. I questioned if I had made a wrong turn and ventured away from God in the last few weeks.

I questioned virtually everything except my faith itself, searching for a reason for my melancholy.
And then I cried.
And then I exhaled.
I confronted the simple fact that the holidays weren't particularly kind to us this year, and after I did, the tears flowed. We started with a very close family member undergoing emergency testing for a likely return of cancer. We followed with cases of the flu, missed exams, canceled Christmas plans, deaths of loved ones, close friends in crises, and a concussion that left me capable of, well, pretty much nothing. Not even writing.
I thought about writing in the midst of all this, but I truly didn't want to just complain in written form, plus the migraines and concussion symptoms prevented me from spending time in front of the computer. None of the cards dealt to me over the holidays were unusual to people who have lived as long as I have. I can see countless faces of others with problems so much bigger than my own. Plus, we still had a lovely Christmas. Truly, we did. Many of the situations are completely resolved now, including the cancer scare. I (mostly) smiled through it all, encouraged others, and kept a positive outlook.
I realized this morning though, during a free-flowing dialogue with God, that although I seemed fine on the outside, I was carrying a great deal of worry and anxiety these last few weeks, burdens I continued to carry today. And I finally just *let it all go*.
I am truly fascinated by my ability to give my worries to God in prayer, and yet somehow still carry them around with me. It's not intentional. For me, it's as if I carry them at the microscopic, cellular level inside my body. Medical scientists have actually proven such a phenomenon exists, and I have to say that for me, my

physical body is intricately and very obviously connected to my emotions, experiences, and thoughts.

I "exhaled," and the relief that flooded me was like a clogged-up channel that broke wide open and began flowing freely again.

We all know life is going to be hard. Curve balls abound. We also know God promises to be with us during tough times.

God is our refuge and strength,
an ever-present help in trouble.
Therefore we will not fear, though the earth give way
and the mountains fall into the heart of the sea,
though its waters roar and foam
and the mountains quake with their surging.
(Ps. 46:1–3)

I wonder though, after the waters still and the quaking stops, what comes next? Do we just keep forging ahead now that the journey looks easier? Do we focus on the past and become bitter or victimized? Do we just keep lugging around all the baggage we just accumulated on that strange, crazy trip life just took us on? I believe when we find ourselves in the calm following the storm, it's vitally important we pause, take a deep breath, and truly exhale. We need to take inventory, count blessings, thank God for answered prayers and lessons learned, and then just release all the pent-up stress, worry, anxiety, and negative feelings.

Everyone instructs us to turn to God in the midst of struggles, and abso-freaking-lutely we should. But I say we shouldn't stop there. When the striving ceases, we need to dive into the Bible. When the trail ends, we need to spend some time alone with the Lord. We need to reflect, pray, worship, journal—whatever brings us closest to the throne room of God.

God longs to speak to us, not only during the dark downpour of a crisis, but also in the calm and stillness after the storm has passed. In the victory. In the release. And let's not forget, in the waiting.

Let's face it. Most of us spend the majority of our lives in what we would classify as the "in-between" times, the day-to-day drudgery, and the repetitive moments of work, eat, sleep. What if we turned over all *those* times to God? How would our relationships with Jesus look? How would our *lives* look? You see, we don't want to be like that one friend that only bothers calling us when they need help or a favor. Meaningful, close relationships involve sharing *everything*, not just catastrophes. Ask yourself what kind of friendship you have with Jesus and what kind of relationship you desire. Don't cheat on God, and don't be only a fair-weather or nasty-weather kind of friend to Him.

> *For the* Lord *your God is a consuming fire, a jealous God.*
> *(Deut. 4:24)*

God desires all of us, all of the time. He is every bit as concerned with our victories as He is with our defeats, with our happiness as our sadness, with our struggles as our ease. Never forget that He pursues us not just when life is difficult, but every moment of every day, even when the skies look clear and the forecast calls for smooth sailing.

Matthew, chapter 8 tells the story of how Jesus calmed an angry, violent sea with a simple word of rebuke. But what happened next, after the tempest passed?

The disciples were amazed and asked, "What kind of man is this? Even the winds and the waves obey him!"
(Matt. 8:27)

Take some time, after the storm passes, to look back and recognize all the Lord has done, and to stand amazed at His power and great faithfulness. Learn the lessons He wanted to teach you, then release the outcome into His capable hands.

Character

Not only so, but we also glory in our sufferings,
because we know that suffering produces perseverance;
perseverance, character
(Rom. 5:3–4a)

FACING CHARACTER

But the fruit of the Spirit [the result of His presence within us] is love [unselfish concern for others], joy, [inner] peace, patience [not the ability to wait, but how we act while waiting], kindness, goodness, faithfulness, gentleness, self-control. Against such things there is no law.
(Gal. 5:22–23, AMP)

One of my pastors, Rev. David Payne, says, "Our happiness isn't God's ultimate goal ... our fruitfulness is." Bearing fruit requires suffering and perseverance, and our character comprises the fruit of those labors. Fruit is an expression of the nature of a tree. When you see ripe, fuzzy peaches hanging from a branch, for example, you know that tree is a peach tree. A peach tree can't produce apples because the tree doesn't choose its own fruit.

Likewise, we are all created uniquely. God has given us a natural bent toward certain abilities, spiritual gifts, and sin. But the more of God, the tree-maker, that we invite into our hearts, minds, and lives, the greater effect He can have on the fruit we produce because He works from the inside out. God does for us that which we cannot do for ourselves: He changes our very nature through the in-dwelling of the Holy Spirit. As this process of internal change develops, we begin to transition from housing rotten, tasteless, or scarce fruit into offering healthy, flavorful, and abundant fruit.

I am the true vine, and my Father is the gardener. He cuts off every branch in me that bears no fruit, while every branch that does bear fruit he prunes so that it will be even more fruitful. You are already clean because of the word I have spoken to you. Remain in me, as I also remain in you. No branch can bear fruit by itself; it must remain in the vine. Neither can you bear fruit unless you remain in me. I am the vine; you are the branches. If you remain in me and I in you, you will bear much fruit; apart from me you can do nothing.
(John 15:1–5)

God is the master of the vineyard. He prunes to bring forth healthier, more abundant fruit and life. How many people can you describe as having tremendous character, who *haven't* faced suffering and yet persevered through it? Instead of praying for ease, we should pray for growth. When that growth occurs, it changes the appearance of our character, and we display the fruits of the Holy Spirit: love, joy, peace, patience, kindness, goodness, faithfulness, gentleness, and self-control.

Dear God,
You are a good, good Father. Thank you for your Holy Spirit. This indescribable gift enables us to be more than we can be on our own. Thank you, Father. Help us to yield to Your pruning as You strive to bring forth abundant life from us. As we seek to claim the character of Jesus for ourselves, help us to turn to You for guidance, strength, and wisdom. May our fruit be fragrant and satisfying to You, O God. May we bask

**in Your grace as we grow in character, for Your glory
and Yours alone.
Amen.**

Additional verses to read about character:
Ephesians 4:1–2
Proverbs 31:10
Philippians 4:8
2 Peter 1:5–7
Colossians 3:12–15

FACING LOVE

I can only show love when I really know how loved I am.[31]
—Steven Curtis Chapman

S itting across from my husband yesterday, I said, "How is it possible that I still love you this much after all these years? I mean, it just keeps *growing!*"

He replied, "I'm like a fungus."

Hands off, ladies, he's mine.

All joking aside, John and I met in a creative writing class in high school. I could not explain the dynamic pull I felt towards this guy. He was not my type at all. This was the dog-eat-dog world of high school cliques. I was a preppy, goody-goody on Student Council, church youth council, varsity tennis and varsity choir; he played soccer, wore black, hard rock concert t-shirts every day with the shirttails out, and wore unkept hair behind his oversized glasses.

I know what you're already thinking, and no, this was not a bad boy attraction. My preoccupation with adult approval would never have allowed room for that. He was really, really intelligent, talented, and creative. He wrote articulate short stories and beautiful songs that left me spellbound.

Something big was happening, and I feared my high school immaturity and concern of what others might think would ruin it. So after he wrote me a letter that started with the words, "God, you are beautiful," I said a prayer that changed both our lives forever. I prayed for God to help me see this young man through *His* eyes. I prayed that I would not be swayed by others' opinions. I prayed for God's will for this just-maybe-beginning relationship.

I kid you not, in that exact moment a "friend" of mine walked over, asked what I was reading, rolled her eyes, and said, "*Please* tell me you're not going out with that guy. Nicki, he's ... you know ... dorky!"

Well-played, God, well-played.

So I fell deeply and truly in love at the young age of 16. By age 19, I was engaged, and by age 20 I was married. We enjoyed a sparkling apple cider toast at our wedding reception because I was not legal to drink champagne! Babies, we were. More than twenty-five years later and we are still happily married.

I can unequivocally say I would choose this man over and over again, every single day; in fact, that's exactly what I do on a daily basis. Love is a choice, often a sacrificial one. Followed by action. On repeat.

> Love is a choice, often a sacrificial one. Followed by action. On repeat.

Despite what greeting card companies, Hollywood movies, and popular music try to tell us, love is not a feeling. It's not the need-to-be-physically-close to someone, tingly feeling in the stomach, heart racing, palms sweating, roller coaster of endorphins. After all, we can experience all this while standing next to a complete stranger (Matthew

McConaughey, anyone?). Feelings come and go, but the Bible tells us that love *remains* (1 Corinthians 13:13).

What does it look like to *remain* in love? Remaining in love looks like:

- giving as much or more than you are receiving;
- greater concern for how you are making the other person feel, rather than how they are making you feel;
- wanting the other person's happiness and well-being, even apart from you;
- gratitude for the smallest of moments together and the largeness of a lifetime together; and
- acknowledgment of a deep love for the other person even in moments when you don't like them very much.

I have always held a great attachment to the love verses in the Bible, 1 Corinthians chapter 13. I thought to myself, here is the blueprint for a lasting relationship right here in Scripture. Few verses spoke so loudly to me at such a young age as these. Insert your own name and those of loved ones within these truths to see if the words ring true. For example, "Nicki is patient and kind. She is not proud or envious." You get the idea.

> *Love is patient, love is kind. It does not envy, it does not boast, it is not proud. It does not dishonor others, it is not self-seeking, it is not easily angered, it keeps no record of wrongs. Love does not delight in evil but rejoices with the truth. It always protects, always trusts, always hopes, always perseveres … And now these three remain: faith, hope and love. But the greatest of these is love.*
> *1 Corinthians 13:4-7, 13*

I will never, ever forget sitting cross-legged on the floor of my teen-aged bedroom, propped up by a giant teddy bear, just a week or so after John and I started dating. I had set my Bible out in front of us, and I read these same verses aloud to him. I wanted him to know this Scripture embodied what I would strive to do in our budding relationship. And then I took a very shaky breath and said, "And I need to tell you now, in case you want to stop dating me, that I'm not going to sleep with you. Not now, not in a few months. Not unless we're married."

All I could hear was my own heart pounding loudly in my ears. My own bravery surprised me, as if it were coming from some place I didn't recognize. He simply replied, "okay."

I was shocked. So I repeated myself. "I'm serious. I will not have sex until I'm married. I understand if that's a deal-breaker. That's a long way off from now. I want you to take some time to think about this. A few days. Then let me know."

"I don't need a few days," he said. "It's okay. I'll wait. *We'll* wait."

Well, if that doesn't speak to a Godly love, I don't know what does. What John gave me in that moment was more than feelings, more than emotion, more than desire. He made a choice. A choice to love like 1 Corinthians 13 instructs us to love. And he followed it with action. On repeat.

The result of loving others in this way is nothing short of remarkable. This is life-changing, miracle-producing stuff, you guys.

When we choose to see others through the eyes of our Heavenly Father, we see the good gifts He has placed inside of them. We see their potential. We see their heart's intent. We see their hurt and their struggles. If we then choose to love and accept them just as they are, we give them the greatest gifts possible: Acceptance. Belonging. Validation. Security.

Never underestimate the power of love to change a life.

> Never underestimate the power of love to change a life.

I think about my son's biological father, who out of love relinquished his parental rights so he could be adopted by us. He wanted his son to have a mom. "Mom" is a word so heavily weighted with love. You see, that man knew that I would take that baby boy to doctor's appointments, soothe him when he was sick or hurt, sit on the floor and play with him, listen to his animated stories, eventually drive him to school, cook him meals, help him with his homework, comfort his broken heart … be his *mom*. And that man also knew that the power of a loving mother can change the entire trajectory of a life. And since he couldn't do those things for his son, he lovingly gave him to a family that could. To us. To me. And *all* our lives were changed for the better because of it.

True, biblical love is an active, powerful force. Love is not a feeling. It is a choice. Often a sacrificial choice. Followed by action. On repeat.

FACING JOY

*Joy is the holy fire that keeps our purpose
warm and our intelligence aglow.*[32]
—Helen Keller

Yesterday morning I sat at the kitchen table with my
Bible and journal, savoring a delicious cup of coffee
and my quiet time with the Lord. I quickly realized it was
not all that quiet, though. After the kids and my husband
had left for the day, I had tidied up the kitchen, loaded
the dishwasher, and turned it on. Next, I had gone into
the laundry room and started a load of bath towels in the
washing machine. The ice maker was emptying its ice
trays and refilling with water, and the air conditioner had
just cycled on, even though it's October. (This is Texas,
y'all. It was ninety-three degrees yesterday, and we were
happy for the *drop* in temps.)

The sounds of all these modern-day machines
prompted me to shoot up a quick "thank you" prayer
to God. I imagined my stay-at-home-mom life without
these conveniences, and I shuddered to think of the
back-breaking labor of my female ancestors. We live
in a remarkable time of ease, and I would have failed
miserably on the frontier. Now, don't get me wrong. I
don't "whistle while I work" all day, every day. I tire

of the never-freaking-ending chores of laundry and kitchen tidying just like the next person. But I do find that my perspective on these labors directly corresponds to the level of satisfaction and—dare I say it, *joy*—that I experience while doing them.

When I remain aware that I perform these and other tasks out of love for my family, I also inwardly recognize that I am doing them for the Lord.

Whatever you do, work at it with all your heart, as working for the Lord, not for human masters, since you know that you will receive an inheritance from the Lord as a reward. It is the Lord Christ you are serving.
(Col. 3:23–24)

I know I often feel as if my work goes unthanked, if not altogether unnoticed. When I begin to dwell on feelings of underappreciation, I remind myself of two things: one, if I'm seeking praise and thanks, then my focus has shifted from God to myself. Two, I'm mistaken if I think that no one sees me. God sees me.

But when you give to the needy, do not let your left hand know what your right hand is doing, so that your giving may be in secret. Then your Father, who sees what is done in secret, will reward you.
(Matt. 6:3–4)

The eyes of the Lord are everywhere, keeping watch on the wicked and the good.
(Prov. 15:3)

The Lord will watch over your coming and going both now and forevermore.
(Ps. 121:8)

God sees us, but it's also crucial that we see Him. A key component to finding joy is learning to recognize Him in all the big and small ways He is trying to reveal Himself to us. I have a friend who started seeing love notes from God in the heart shapes she found in nature. Since she shared this practice with me, I see them everywhere now too. Ask God to show you His presence, and He will!

We can also find joy by inviting and welcoming Him into even the most mundane moments of our days. We can pray without ceasing. We can say "thank you, God" for the small things as well as the big things. We can seek God's perspective on our current situations, and ask to see others through His eyes.

Ruth Chou Simons says in *Beholding and Becoming, the Art of Everyday Worship,* that "We become joyful and glad about *this* day—today—as we take our eyes off of what we must do and behold the One who created us to do it in the first place."[33]

Shifting our focus away from our circumstances and toward Father God elicits joy.

> *Though you have not seen him, you love him;*
> *and even though you do not see him now, you believe*
> *in him and are filled with an inexpressible and glorious joy,*
> *for you are receiving the end result of your faith,*
> *the salvation of your souls.*
> *(1 Pet. 1:8–9)*

Our faith in Him also produces joy, and that joy becomes our strength.

Nehemiah said, "Go and enjoy choice food and
sweet drinks, and send some to those who have nothing
prepared. This day is holy to our Lord. Do not grieve, for the
joy of the LORD is your strength."
(Neh. 8:10)

Our faith
in Him also
produces
joy, and that
joy becomes
our strength.

Have you ever watched
someone go through a painful
ordeal and marveled at his or
her ability to maintain a smile
and joyful attitude through it
all? I've watched a friend of
mind walk through leukemia
and bone marrow transplant
protocols. She calls every nurse,
nurse assistant, phlebotomist,
lab tech, and transporter by name, and asks them personal
questions when she sees them. Their names are on her
prayer list that she pours over daily. A steady stream of
interruptions breezes into her hospital room, and she
greets each one with a smile. They poke and prod her
tired body while she remembers to ask if so-and-so's son
passed his reading test last week. She amazes me. My
friend's type of joy does not come from personal strength;
it comes from God. When we have faith in a good and
perfect God and we put ourselves firmly in His hands
and under His authority, He releases a joy, security, and
peace in us that defies our circumstances.

When I'm finding it difficult to locate that spring of
joy within, I change my words until my heart and mind
can catch up. I reframe statements like "I have to" into "I
get to," and "I'm so glad that ..." into "thank you, God,
that...," and from "Please, God ..." into "God, you are
...." If we can change our words, our minds will follow,
and then our perspective changes to that of God's. Seeing

our circumstances through His eyes develops an eternal mindset in us that will release the joy of His presence into our lives.

Whether we're fighting cancer, driving carpool, arguing a case, teaching young minds, or doing household chores like me, Jesus is our companion. If we will tap into His presence and express gratitude for it, an unmistakable joy will well up inside us. It's a joy not defined by our circumstances. And just like the laundry, it's a never-ending well that won't run dry.

FACING PEACE

When peace, like a river, attendeth my way,
When sorrows like sea billows roll;
Whatever my lot, Thou hast taught me to say,
It is well, it is well, with my soul.[34]
—"It Is Well With My Soul" by Horatio Spafford

"**M**oooommmmyyyyy," came the sing-song voice from my toddler's bedroom as he woke up from his afternoon nap. "I have a supwiiiiise for youuuuuu!"

I opened the door to the nursery and smiled at his cherubic face, standing on bare legs with one tiny, fisted hand outstretched to me. He was both fully awake and fully intent on the mission in his hand.

He smiled brightly up at me and said, "Heww Mommy! I have a pwesent fo you!"

"You do?" I said enthusiastically, and absent-mindedly held out my hand while he deposited his tiny gift there.

He exclaimed triumphantly, "It's poop!"

I looked down at my open hand, and sure enough, there lay a toddler-sized black turd that he had stolen from the depths of his diaper. It was a surprise, alright. Just not one that I wanted. Oh, the twists and turns of parenthood. Everything can be going swimmingly one minute, and the very next you are literally holding a load of crap in your hands.

These sudden changes are not just limited to parenthood, though. This is *life*, right? One minute you are just rocking right along, and then suddenly the phone rings and you get the tragic news that a loved one has died. Maybe you feel amazing and have been exercising, but then you get a call from the doctor saying your bloodwork looks suspicious and you need to come in for tests because they suspect cancer. Maybe you and your teen seem to be getting along well, and he's doing well in school, but then you find a stash of empty beer cans in the garage from a secret party. Sometimes, seemingly out of nowhere, chaos erupts. And what do we do? Well, if you're anything like me, you probably panic.

In fact, that's what Jesus's disciples did, too. I am reminded of the story in Mark, chapter 4, of how Jesus calmed the storm. The disciples were out on the water and all was well—until suddenly it wasn't. The wind shifted, and the surf swelled; rain pelted down, and the men called for all-hands-on-deck as a sudden, violent storm erupted. Chaos ensued. What did the disciples do? They panicked! Racing around trying to right the boat and bail water, they suddenly remembered that Jesus was there, because they saw him *sleeping* in the stern.

Jesus was in the stern, sleeping on a cushion. The disciples woke him and said to him, "Teacher, don't you care if we drown?" He got up, rebuked the wind and said to the waves, "Quiet! Be still!" Then the wind died down and it was completely calm. He said to his disciples, "Why are you so afraid? Do you still have no faith?"
(Mark 4:38–40)

We can learn so many lessons from this story. First, God allowed a storm to challenge the disciples. They weren't spared because they followed Jesus. The storm hit, and it hit hard. Why, you ask? So that God's power—through Jesus Christ—could be displayed. Because of this, the disciples' faith increased.

Second, where was Jesus during the storm? He was right there in the middle of it, close to His disciples. He did not abandon them, nor was He flummoxed by the pandemonium. Likewise, we must know that Jesus remains close to us during our storms too.

Third, all the disciples needed to do was call out to Jesus, and He spoke peace into their situation. In this case, the physical storm instantly calmed. For us, Jesus may calm our storm by removing a difficult situation, or He might calm our souls and spirits within that situation when we rest and trust in Him. In both cases, peace enters our circumstances when we fix our eyes on Jesus instead of the disturbance. Finding peace in the midst of our storms requires a conscious recognition that Jesus is walking right beside us, and that we are not facing anything that we—or others—haven't faced before.

My pastor, Rev. David Payne, posed this question to us recently during worship. He asked, "How many times must we panic in the chaos before we trust in God—in His power, His strength, and His goodness? How many times must we panic before we look back and see His faithfulness in the past and realize He is also with us now?" It's a question we should all ask ourselves. Is our first reaction to panic or to pray? Through prayer, we shift our focus from the daunting waves surrounding us to the one who calms the storm. We leave behind fears and worries and grab hold of trust and faith.

But the Advocate, the Holy Spirit, whom the Father will send in my name, will teach you all things and will remind you of everything I have said to you. Peace I leave with you; my peace I give you. I do not give to you as the world gives. Do not let your hearts be troubled and do not be afraid.
(John 14:26–27)

Sit still in the eye of your storm and meditate on God's presence, steadfastness, and strength. Know the difference between seeking the peace *of* God, and seeking to be at peace *with* God. The latter requires intimacy and relationship with Him.

Be strong and courageous. Do not be afraid or terrified because of them, for the Lord your God goes with you; he will never leave you nor forsake you.
(Deut. 31:6)

Take a look backward and see the ways His grace and mercy have saved you before. Allow His peace to overcome your panic. Take note of His presence and guidance through difficult times in the past and thank Him, trusting He will do the same now and in the future—even on the days you're left holding a handful of poop.

> Know the difference between seeking the peace *of* God, and seeking to be at peace *with* God.

FACING PATIENCE

You can get so confused
that you'll start in to race
down long wiggled roads at a break-necking pace
and grind on for miles cross weirdish wild space,
headed, I fear, toward a most useless place.
The Waiting Place ...[35]
—*Oh! The Places You'll Go* by Dr. Seuss

S team rose from the shower as hot water pelted my
skin. Gut-wracking sobs convulsed from my body as
I curled into a ball on the tile floor and screamed out to
God, "Please, *please*, let me know You are here. I can't
do it any longer without You, God. I need to feel Your
presence, please. I can't go on like this."

Anguish seeped from every pore in my body. I had
been in pain for months and practically bed-ridden,
unable to drive, cook, complete everyday tasks, or care
for my family. Far worse than the physical pain I was
suffering from, was the emotional and spiritual pain: God
had hidden Himself from me. I knew He was with me.
He hadn't moved. But He wasn't allowing me to feel His
comfort or His presence. I could no longer hear His voice.
I knew He was teaching me, allowing me to go through

this dark valley. It was the loneliest, emptiest void I have ever experienced.

I prayed through Scripture constantly, saying, "God, I know your word says 'You will never leave me nor forsake me.' Help to believe it." I journaled and pleaded with God, "Increase my faith. Allow me to feel the joy of Your presence once again." I labored with the Lord for over a year, seeking healing and wholeness.

But for a time, the only answer was silence—until that day in the shower. When I truly reached a point of desperation, His Holy Spirit came rushing back in like a warm embrace from a loving Father, cradling His scared and wounded child. I did not receive physical healing in that moment but, rather, spiritual healing. The joy of His presence had returned.

There may be a time when you question if God is near. Sometimes we wander away from Him, from the protection that He provides when we are operating in the center of His will for our lives. Other times, He's like a father taking His hand off the back of the bicycle seat of His child's first two-wheeler. He's still running right alongside that bike, but for a moment, He releases His hand so we know what it is like to ride alone.

When we are in the midst of a period of suffering, in the middle of a mess of tears and brokenness, where is God? He's right there in the waiting. I hate to disagree with the master wordsmith we call Dr. Seuss, but "the waiting place" is *not* useless. The waiting place is where God does some of His best work in us, and where He teaches us the gift of patience.

One of my favorite songs, "Take Courage," sung by Kristene DiMarco of Bethel Music, puts it this way:

> *Sing praise my soul, find strength in joy*
> *Let His words lead you on*

Do not forget His great faithfulness
He'll finish all He's begun.
So take courage my heart.
Stay steadfast my soul.
He's in the waiting. He's in the waiting.
Hold onto your hope as your triumph unfolds.
He's never failing. He's never failing.[36]

Our heavenly Father's eyes are always on the end game. Our redemption. *All* of our redemption. Mankind. Humankind. His glorious creation.

"For my thoughts are not your thoughts, neither are your ways my ways," declares the Lord. "As the heavens are higher than the earth, so are my ways higher than your ways and my thoughts than your thoughts."
(Isa. 55:8–9)

For me, the hard part of patience is waiting with *expectancy* instead of *expectation*. Eric Johnson of Bethel Church once said that expectancy is waiting without a timeline or deadline.[37] We wait with hope and trust. When we assign criteria or deadlines to what we will accept as God's answer to our prayers, we are actually testing Him. We are limiting God to our own timeline and understanding. We are trying to define Him instead of allowing Him to define us. And faith—real, deep, abiding faith—isn't really faith if we only believe when everything is going well and according to our schedules. Those so-called schedules are the very definition of impatience. They are feeble attempts at controlling our own lives, rather than acknowledging God is in control of them.

As we struggle with patience, most of us will have questions, and what are we to do with those? Ask God your questions! Often our questions drive us deeper into His

Word, into worship of Him, into prayer, and into consultation with Christian mentors; these are all things God desires for us. While we wait and search for comfort and understanding, He meets us right where we are, and our relationship with Him strengthens. God makes great use of our time in "the waiting place," and we can and should lean into Him when we find ourselves there.

Ruth Chou Simons says in *Gracelaced,* "When one chapter closes and another is still not ours, the beauty we get to experience is seeing how the Father provides in the now and not yet."[38] God will do what God wants to do when God deems the time is right. Our job is to trust in His goodness, His plans, and His presence—in the here, the now, and the not yet—right smack dab in the middle of the crying. He's in the waiting. He is right here with us.

> When we assign criteria or deadlines to what we will accept as God's answer to our prayers, we are actually testing Him. We are limiting God to our own timeline and understanding.

And His final act? It's going to be better than we can even imagine. Practice patience, my friends, because it's totally going to be worth the wait.

FACING KINDNESS

There are three ways to ultimate success:
The first way is to be kind.
The second way is to be kind.
The third way is to be kind.[39]
—Mister Rogers

Toddlerhood came tearing through my house accompanied by the sounds of a slightly older sister whining and tattling.

"Mom! The potty won't flush, and Johnathan won't give my Polly Pocket doll back to me! You said he's not allowed to play with them! He keeps running away from me, and I don't know where my doll is."

Wait. Back up. The potty won't flush? *Red warning lights flashing.*

Yep. You guessed it. Polly Pocket had succumbed to a watery toilet death.

Talk about a costly funeral. A call to the plumber, a service call to the house, a horrible prognosis, a second service call to the house, and one brand-spanking-new toilet later, and I considered the situation finally (albeit expensively) resolved. Until, of course, my daughter came to me, asking for her cherished doll.

"Did the plumbers find her?" she implored.

Honestly, the tiny, plastic plaything was the last issue on my mind. I hadn't even considered that my clean-freak child would *want* the toy back, knowing it had taken a toilet dive. Then, I remembered how important that little doll was to my sweet girl, even though I couldn't personally understand the attachment.

"No, sweetie," I answered. "They couldn't get her. They had to push her out into the open sewer line."

Tears began to fill the corners of her crystal blue eyes, and then visions of *Finding Nemo* surfaced in her little mind, and she brightened.

"So ... she's swimming in the ocean now?"

I considered answering truthfully, but images of her doll floating in a pool of raw sewage for infinity seemed a terrible fate, so I settled on a kinder response.

"Yes, honey. She's a mermaid now!"

Looking back, my maternal white lie begs the question: What does kindness really look like? And, is there a cost?

The story of the good Samaritan provides an excellent example of kindness. A Jewish man was robbed and beaten, left bleeding on the side of the road, when another Jewish man passed by and ignored the injured man's pleas for help. Eventually, a Samaritan man walked by and stopped to render aid. The Samaritan bandaged the Jewish man's wounds and paid for a place where the wounded man could stay and recuperate.

The Jewish man who passed by and continued on his way likely assumed the victim was a member of an unclean sect, like a Samaritan, when in fact, the victim was a fellow Jew. If a Jewish man had stopped to help and had touched a Samaritan, his religion stated he would be "unclean" and untouchable himself for a designated period of time. Jesus turns this story around for His listeners by illustrating that it was an "unclean" Samaritan who bothered to help a victimized Jew, and the Jew who passed by was actually hurting himself and his "own kind" by failing to render aid, due to his own prejudices and religious rules.

Like the Jew in this story that passes the victim by, we too sometimes use religion or Scripture to excuse or justify ourselves for not extending kindness or mercy to others, especially when the "others" fall into easily-segregated groups of people.

> My Father's house has many rooms;
> if that were not so, would I have told you that
> I am going there to prepare a place for you?
> (John 14:2)

Jesus declared He has prepared a place for us *all*. There is room for us *all*. We do not need to shove others aside or compete for scraps under His communion table. The kingdom of God is a rich, vibrant tapestry of color and tongues; if it were not so, why would He have formed us in such diverse ways? We do not need to compete for our heavenly Father's affection; in fact, He instructs us to do the opposite.

The essence of kindness is this: care for one another, encourage one another, and help one another.

For the entire law is fulfilled in keeping this one command: "Love your neighbor as yourself."
(Gal. 5:14)

Love and embrace all, for we are all His creation, fashioned in His own image. The essence of kindness is this: care for one another, encourage one another, and help one another. Jesus modeled this perfectly for us by touching and healing the lepers, eating with tax collectors, and conversing with ostracized women and sinners.

Today, kindness looks like reaching across the political aisle with tolerance and acceptance. It looks like the church forfeiting ideas of "this is how we've always done it" in favor of "this seems to resonate with the unchurched." It looks like truly listening to those with different viewpoints and experiences, rather than speaking over them or diminishing their perspectives. It looks like serving others, rather than being catered to or served. It looks like us defining ourselves by what we are "*for*" rather than what we are "*against.*"

Kindness looks like:

- mercy, not condemnation;
- acceptance, not ridicule;
- empathy, not apathy;
- diversity, not uniformity;
- patience, not agitation; and
- action, not words.

Those who consider themselves religious and yet
do not keep a tight rein on their tongues deceive themselves,
and their religion is worthless. Religion that God our Father
accepts as pure and faultless is this: to look after orphans
and widows in their distress and to keep oneself from being
polluted by the world.
(James 1:26–27)

It's not easy to avoid being "polluted by the world." Truthfully, it's easier to focus on differences, aggravations, and grievances. The cost of kindness may very well be a degree of discomfort. But when we offer kindness to one another, we can all experience the benefits of feeling seen and heard. Mister Rogers said, "The world needs a sense of worth, and it will achieve it only by its people feeling that they are worthwhile."[40] Kindness and empathy change lives. Therefore, strive to be kind to everyone with whom you come into contact. In doing so, you just might change the world.

FACING GOODNESS

The best-laid schemes o' Mice an' Men
Gang aft a-gley[41]
—Robert Burns

Good intentions. They often go hand-in-hand with regrets. Robert Burn's lines from *To a Mouse* are often misquoted as "The best laid plans of mice and men often go awry." And oh, how true it is.

Recently, my husband and I got up early on a Saturday to watch our daughter play tennis and then attend the wedding of our good friends' daughter. The tennis matches lasted much longer than we anticipated, and it was blisteringly hot outside. Our daughter finished way past lunchtime, and none of us had eaten. So we came home, fed our bellies, took showers to get the sweat and stink off, and propped ourselves up in bed for thirty minutes in the cool air conditioning to take a break before getting dressed for the wedding.

You guessed it. We fell asleep. And we slept through the entire wedding. Imagine going to your friends and saying, "We're very sorry we missed the biggest day of your daughter's life. We took a nap instead." Ouch. Good intentions, followed by hurt and regret.

Numerous authors and philosophers have stated throughout time, that most of the evil in this world is done by people with good intentions. I must agree. How many times have I intervened in an argument between my children only to hear, "But I didn't *mean* to hurt her feelings, Mom!" It's as if the absence of the intent to do harm excuses the outcome. Uh, no, kiddo. My response to such a statement is always this, "It doesn't matter if you meant to or not because you *did* hurt her feelings. Whether you meant to or not, she is hurt. And when you hurt someone, you apologize."

Meaning well and doing well are entirely different things. Meaning well doesn't amount to much—except in the eyes of our heavenly Father. Hear these reassuring words:

> But the LORD said to Samuel, "Do not consider his appearance or his height, for I have rejected him. The LORD does not look at the things people look at. People look at the outward appearance, but the LORD looks at the heart."
> (1 Sam. 16:7)

Oh, sweet salvation and mercy. We may not all be going to hell in a hand-basket after all. Why? Because our heavenly Father cares about our good intentions. He cares about what's in our hearts. King David was credited as a man after God's heart, and yet he committed adultery and murder. Mary, sister of Martha, allowed her sister to do all the work of entertaining and feeding Jesus and His followers, while she sat at Jesus's feet, doing supposedly nothing. Mary did *what*, you say? She *sat*! And Jesus said Mary had made the better choice, to simply sit and learn from the Master.

John Wesley, one of the founders of the Methodist church, is frequently misquoted as saying, "Do all the good you can, by all the means you can, in all the ways you can, in all the places you can, at all the times you can, to all the people you can, as long as ever you can." Experts on John Wesley claim they can find no evidence that he ever uttered these words. Regardless of its origins, I feel overwhelmed just reading the statement. In a world obsessed with action and results, God has sent the unusual message that He cares about sentiment, intention, and potential. That's not to say that we should ignore John Wesley's general instructions to live out our faith in service to God and others, but we should remember that those activities are not stamps on a frequent flyer pass that will get us into heaven. Only Jesus can accomplish our salvation, and only the Holy Spirit's goodness, poured into us, can cause us to do good for others.

I don't know about you, but sometimes, despite a heart full of good intentions, I mess things up in spectacular fashion. I hate feeling like every option available to me will only make a situation worse, as if it's unfixable. I am utterly miserable when I feel a person on the other side of a contentious situation has already made up his or her mind about my intent, and nothing I can do or say will change it. On those days, all I can do is rest in the knowledge that God truly sees me, loves me, and forgives me. When I am embarrassed and feeling like an utter failure, I try to remind myself of the following verse:

For I am convinced that neither death nor life,
neither angels nor demons, neither the present nor the future,
nor any powers, neither height nor depth, nor anything else
in all creation, will be able to separate us from the love of God
that is in Christ Jesus our Lord.
(Rom. 8:38–39)

There is nothing I can ever do that can separate me from the love of Christ. No failure on my part will ever tarnish the goodness of Jesus. And *my* goodness? It comes from Him, not my track record of good deeds, so I keep leaning into Him and aiming to be kind to others, all the while praying that He will bring beauty out of the messes I make. I think the key to possessing goodness is to not just live out all our Holy-Spirit-guided good intentions, but to also consistently draw nearer to God and allow His goodness to transform our hearts and minds.

His divine power has given us everything we need for a godly life through our knowledge of him who called us by his own glory and goodness.
(2 Pet. 1:3)

We need to remember we can never be "good enough" on our own. Any goodness we possess comes from God.

Why do you think so many worship songs speak of God's goodness? Because we forget that the very nature of God is good, and because we are acutely aware of how *not good* we ourselves are! We need to remember we can never be "good enough" on our own. Any goodness we possess comes from God.

Every good and perfect gift is from above, coming down from the Father of the heavenly lights, who does not change like shifting shadows.
(James 1:17)

Take the time, make the call, send the note, sign up to volunteer, and be truly present with others; but most importantly, turn to God and remember His goodness. And when you screw it all up, as we all will from time to time, just apologize and keep moving forward. Gaze constantly into the face of our good, good Father. And live out those good intentions, for goodness' sake.

FACING FAITHFULNESS

Nothing formed against me shall stand
You hold the whole world in your hands
I'm holding on to your promises
You are faithful
You are faithful[42]
—"Whom Shall I Fear" by Chris Tomlin

One typical Sunday afternoon at home while the whole family busied themselves with various activities, my pre-school-aged son suddenly entered the living room and yelled: "I need *peace* and *quiet*! Only *me* is allowed to talk or whistle!"

Everyone immediately got quiet, exchanged perplexed glances with each other, and then burst out laughing. Peace and quiet would not exist while he was talking and whistling, but the irony of the command was completely lost on its pint-sized speaker. He stormed out of the room, frustrated that the rest of the family wasn't obeying his every dictate.

I think we often confuse obedience with faithfulness. By definition, obedience involves submitting to an authority of some kind; faithfulness is an unwavering devotion to a person or idea. Obedience involves more action, and faithfulness more emotion. The idea of faithfulness in marriage, for example, involves *both:* the action of upholding one's vows, and adhering emotionally to one's spouse and to the idea of marriage.

As Christians, faithfulness to God looks like heart-felt devotion as well as obedience or action, similar to the marriage example above. How many times have we heard the words "faithful follower" used to describe a human pillar of the Christian community? So it stands to reason that if we believe in God and give Him authority in our life, our faithfulness to Him looks like active obedience to Christ's teachings. To be faithful, one must follow, or surrender one's own will.

Then (Jesus) said to them all:
"Whoever wants to be my disciple must deny themselves
and take up their cross daily and follow me."
(Luke 9:23)

In a society that prides itself on innovation and leadership, "following" doesn't come naturally. We want to take charge, not surrender. We want to lead, not follow. We want to give orders, not obey them. As always, we can look to Jesus Himself for the perfect example of faithfulness.

Going a little farther, he fell with his face to the ground
and prayed, "My Father, if it is possible, may this cup be
taken from me. Yet not as I will, but as you will."
(Matt. 26:39)

Jesus understood His purpose from the beginning of time. He foretold His death numerous times while He walked the earth. Still, in the moments before His physical agony would begin, He prayed for Father God's will to take precedence over His own. That's how faithfulness— and obedience—look in real life.

Although our own stories may look less dramatic than His, we are called to the same kind of faithfulness as Jesus. However, the real beauty and mystery of faithfulness is that we can't attain it. At least not on our own.

Paul explains in Galatians how, through faith in Christ, we are no longer slaves to maintaining the letter of the law through obedience, but rather the Holy Spirit can achieve for us what we ourselves cannot: a changed nature.

You, my brothers and sisters, were called to be free. But do not use your freedom to indulge the flesh; rather, serve one another humbly in love … So I say, walk by the Spirit, and you will not gratify the desires of the flesh. For the flesh desires what is contrary to the Spirit, and the Spirit what is contrary to the flesh. They are in conflict with each other, so that you are not to do whatever you want. But if you are led by the Spirit, you are not under the law.
(Gal. 5:13, 16–18)

Verse 24 goes on to explain that those who profess faith in Christ Jesus have "crucified the flesh with its passions and desires," meaning we can overcome our sinful natures with the in-dwelling help of the Holy Spirit. That same Holy Spirit will lead us into faithfulness to God.

This is good news, people. We *all* struggle with sin and unfaithfulness to the law and to Christ's teachings. But with the arrival of our Messiah, Jesus, who is the fulfillment of the law, we are no longer subject to the old law. Hear His own words in the following verse.

Do not think that I have come to abolish the Law or the Prophets; I have not come to abolish them but to fulfill them.
(Matt. 5:17)

Jesus is the new covenant, and that covenant is based on God's love for us, not on what we do for Him. For a recovering perfectionist like myself, that sounds a lot like freedom.

> Not that we are competent in ourselves to
> claim anything for ourselves, but our competence
> comes from God. He has made us competent as ministers
> of a new covenant—not of the letter but of the Spirit;
> for the letter kills, but the Spirit gives life.
> (2 Cor. 3:5–6)

Faithfulness looks like:

- loving others, not condemning them;
- devotion to Jesus, not religion;
- heart knowledge, not head knowledge;
- a deep need for God, not self-sufficiency;
- Jesus as the way to heaven, not self-righteousness; and
- boasting in His forgiveness, not a list of good deeds.

It all runs contrary to our normal way of thinking, doesn't it? But God has a knack for flipping our world upside down, and Jesus was famous for saying the opposite of what everyone expected Him to say.

Time and again in the Bible, Jesus refuted the Pharisees' legalism in favor of love and mercy. This was *His* brand of faithfulness. And it should be ours too. Jesus was faithful to His mission to save the lost

Jesus is the new covenant, and that covenant is based on God's love for us, not on what we do for Him.

and redeem mankind. Jesus was faithful to His calling to sacrifice Himself for us. Jesus was faithful to being a living example of the character of God.

We are called to be faithful as well—faithful followers of the New Covenant, of Jesus Christ—not to fulfill the letter of the law, but to love and live as He did. God wants more than our obedience, my friends. He wants our whole-hearted devotion to Him. He wants our faithfulness.

FACING GENTLENESS

Nothing is so strong as gentleness,
nothing so gentle as real strength.[43]
—Saint Francis de Sales

M y husband, youngest daughter, and I sat curled up on the bed, trying to watch a TV show. I said "trying," because our son was taking a bath in the next room, and per his usual routine, he was methodically working his way through the personal "greatest hits of Johnathan" at scream-level volume.

John, laughing, said, "Can you hear our son singing in the bathtub?"

I replied, "Well, that's not exactly *singing!*"

To which our daughter added, "He sounds like a constipated mockingbird."

She's hysterical but—bless her heart—gentle answers are not always her strong suit. She's more of an unfiltered, tell-it-like-it-is kind of girl.

Gentleness, according to Scripture, is one of the fruits of the Spirit. I dare say we enter this world with gentler tendencies than we possess by the time we're adults. Young children often express seemingly innate gentleness toward babies, animals, and children younger than themselves. It's difficult, though, to find gentle souls and demeanors in adults; it's as if the world has beaten the tenderness right out of us. One can simply pull up any social media app and immediately find an unending discourse of everything *but* gentle dialogue. It is fashionable and trendy to be harried, stressed, frustrated, catty, and even angry. Outrage over everything from parking spots to politics is the new "cool." In the media and political sphere in America, in particular, we operate in a state of contempt for others, fostering an "us versus them" mentality in which anyone who disagrees with us is a "them" and must be demonized and vilified. Our behavior is a far cry from the gentleness that Jesus modeled for us.

Remember the story of the woman at the well, found in John, chapter 4, of the Bible? The woman was a Samaritan, and Jesus was a Jew, meaning the two of them were forbidden to interact with one another. Jesus asked her for a drink from the well, explained that He could offer her living water, and asked her to go and get her husband and bring him back. Jesus knew fully well the woman was a Samaritan. He also knew she'd already had five husbands and that the man she was currently involved with was not her spouse. He spoke gently and kindly to her, first about the task she was doing and second about her life; He did this to gain her attention and understanding. Jesus didn't approach her and then start shouting at her about her sins and mistakes.

I think we Christians (read: "Jesus followers") are often guilty of taking the latter approach, instead of the one Jesus modeled for us. We eagerly and loudly point out all the things we are "against" and angry about, rather than drawing others to God through the beautiful, loving, merciful story of Jesus Christ. We need to be reminded of the adage, "You can catch more flies with honey than with vinegar." Gentleness goes a long way.

Remind the people to be subject to rulers
and authorities, to be obedient, to be ready to do whatever is
good, to slander no one, to be peaceable and considerate, and
always to be gentle toward everyone.
(Titus 3:1–2)

Notice in this verse that Paul does not instruct us to *agree* with everyone, but he does tell us to be peaceable, gentle, respectful, and courteous. If the CIA were to do a deep dive of all your interactions with others, including those on social media and online, could they say you live up to Paul's guidelines in the verse above? Furthermore, would you truly want to live up to them, or do you sometimes take pride in acting brash, disobedient, or argumentative? I ask this because I think we have a fundamental misunderstanding of what gentleness, in biblical terms, means. Most males, especially, eschew notions of gentleness in favor of some version of machismo. As females, we struggle and fight for equality and don't want to be seen as weak. None of these things could be said of the world's only perfect person, though: Jesus.

To better understand just what gentleness means, let's look at the word *meekness*, an often-used synonym for gentleness. In fact, in Galatians 5, the Greek word we've translated as "gentleness" is more closely translated from the Greek as "meekness." Wikipedia defines meekness as "righteous, humble, teachable, and patient under suffering; willing to follow gospel teachings … restraining one's own power, so as to allow room for others."

I don't know about you, but I don't see a whole lot of people these days restraining their power so they can allow room for others to grab some! And yet, this is what the Bible asks of us: to put others ahead of ourselves and to follow the gentle example of Christ in all our interactions.

No one should seek their own good, but the good of others.
(1 Cor. 10:24)

I experienced a wonderful example of gentleness recently at the hands of my "constipated mockingbird." I was having a particularly difficult and emotional day. My son was sitting next to me on the couch and said, "Mom, are you going to cry?" I replied, "I already am, a little." And he said, "It's OK, Mom, you can cry on me." And with those words, he snuggled up really close and gently placed his tweenaged arm around me.

This is what the Bible asks of us: to put others ahead of ourselves and to follow the gentle example of Christ in all our interactions.

Therefore, as God's chosen people, holy and dearly loved, clothe yourselves with compassion, kindness, humility, gentleness and patience.
(Col. 3:12)

I think we can all agree we would like others to treat us gently, just as my son did for me. Each of us is, after all, fighting battles others may not know about. We are all different versions of broken, yet how often do we criticize others for expressing their emotions, rather than gently moving in closer, being available to them, and giving the Holy Spirit a chance to show us their perspective?

As a prisoner for the Lord, then, I urge you to live a life worthy of the calling you have received. Be completely humble and gentle; be patient, bearing with one another in love.
(Eph. 4:1–2)

Gentleness can take many forms. As my son exhibited, it can simply look like listening and giving others a safe space to express their feelings. As the apostle Peter tells us in 1 Peter 3:4, a gentle and quiet spirit is very precious to our heavenly Father, and its beauty will never fade. Being gentle with others will cost us nothing, but it will enable us to gain valuable relationships and understanding.

FACING SELF-CONTROL

Mommy, I'm mad wiff you.
—Johnathan Carlson, age 3

I'm mad at my husband. That's difficult for me to even say because this is a pretty rare occurrence. I am married to an actual treasure of a man, a loving and devoted spouse, but right now, I'm angry. Yesterday I traveled out of town to see a specialist and undergo a minor surgical procedure. I was nervous and uncertain, but I drove myself. I'm pretty sure my husband forgot the procedure was even happening. After some uncomfortable tests, the doctor came in the room and said I did not need the scheduled procedure after all. I was elated! I had prayed for this very outcome. But then the doctor recommended a CT scan. Multiple treatment options were given, and I just rather blindly chose one. More waiting, another test, and eventually the doctor entered the room where I was waiting and started discussing surgical options. Real surgery this time. My elation turned quickly into despair. And still, I sat alone, trying to process all the information the doctor was quickly throwing at me.

I texted my husband and received a two-word reply. I texted again and could tell from the response that he was involved with something at work. He asked to talk later. I swallowed my tears and fears and got in the car for the thirty-minute-drive home. The entire day passed without my husband reaching out to me. When we saw each other later that night, it seemed he had forgotten the entire situation all over again. We were at Bible study, so I said simply that I was hurt, and we would have to wait to discuss it. The entire night passed without so much as a conversation. No "Are you okay?" or "What did the doctor say?" Nothing. I could tell he had other things on his mind, but I was angry that I was not one of them.

I don't know a single person that hasn't struggled with anger at some point. How we deal with it varies greatly, though. Some get vengeful and violent. Others get stoic. Still others cry. I think for all of us, anger sparks a war between sin and self-control.

In your anger do not sin: Do not let the sun go down while
you are still angry, and do not give the devil a foothold.
(Eph. 4:26–27)

My mind spun scenarios all day long of little ways to express my hurt, and of snide remarks I could say to call my beloved's attention to his actions (or lack thereof). Part of me wanted to hurt his feelings in return, but I knew *expressing* my pain and *addressing* my pain were very different things. I did not want to argue, and I did not want to say things I might regret. Instead, I held my tongue.

A gentle answer turns away wrath,
but a harsh word stirs up anger.
(Prov. 15:1)

I often tell my son, "It's okay to be mad. It's not okay to hurt others because of it, though." The first statement is a fact of human nature; the second involves self-control. We all get angry, but that does not give us license to sin in our anger. God expects self-control from us.

Despite wanting to lash out, yell, and cry, I noticed myself doing some kind things while still in the throes of my pity party. First, my husband texted me, asking if I could bring his tablet to church for him, and I did. While we were eating supper in the fellowship hall, I got up to get dessert, and I picked up a dessert for him as well and brought it to him. When we prayed, I reached out and held his hand. When I retrieved a stick of gum from my purse, I silently offered him a piece also.

Now, I didn't do these things out of habit, because I was drowning in my hurt feelings and found myself not wanting to do nice things for him. On the contrary, I made very conscious choices to offer these kindnesses to him, but only after praying for God to help me control my actions.

> So I say, walk by the Spirit, and you will not gratify the
> desires of the flesh. For the flesh desires what is contrary
> to the Spirit, and the Spirit what is contrary to the flesh.
> They are in conflict with each other, so that you are not to
> do whatever you want ... But the fruit of the Spirit is love,
> joy, peace, forbearance, kindness, goodness, faithfulness,
> gentleness and self-control. Against such things there is no
> law. Those who belong to Christ Jesus have crucified the flesh
> with its passions and desires.
> (Gal. 5:16–17, 22–24)

Notice the Scriptures do not say these are the fruits of *me* or the fruits of *you*. These traits come from the indwelling of the Holy Spirit. We can't do this on our own. I wanted to be ugly and vengeful. Only after many quickly-uttered, in-the-moment prayers did I manage to say nothing at all. And friends, prayer may be the most useful weapon we can wield in the battle of sin versus self-control. Another weapon in our arsenal is the Word of God.

My dear brothers and sisters, take note of this:
Everyone should be quick to listen, slow to speak and slow
to become angry, because human anger does not produce the
righteousness that God desires. Therefore, get rid of all moral
filth and the evil that is so prevalent and humbly accept the
word planted in you, which can save you. Do not merely
listen to the word, and so deceive yourselves. Do what it says.
(James 1:19-22)

The Word made flesh and the Word of the Scripture are one and the same: Jesus Christ. Jesus, while both human and divine, did not sin. If we can learn to respond, behave, and speak as Jesus did, we will exhibit self-control. If we allow the gift of the Holy Spirit to dwell within us, it will guide us through our battles against our flesh.

Watch and pray so that you will
not fall into temptation.
The spirit is willing, but the
flesh is weak.
(Matt. 26:41)

If we allow the gift of the Holy Spirit to dwell within us, it will guide us through our battles against our flesh.

Today, I feel my need to express my hurt feelings lessening and the need to address them growing. This morning before leaving for work, my husband asked if we could have lunch together today. He said he wants to listen to me and talk everything through. We will start our conversation with prayer and allow the Holy Spirit to guide us as we have many times in the past.

Those who live according to the flesh have their minds set on what the flesh desires; but those who live in accordance with the Spirit have their minds set on what the Spirit desires.
(Rom. 8:5)

Self-control is truly a misnomer. We don't control ourselves. Rather, the grace of God changing our hearts and desires, and the Holy Spirit prompting us when and how to act, ultimately directs our behavior. Ironically, the way to win the battle of self-control is to completely surrender—surrender ourselves wholly to God and His Holy Spirit.

FACING AUTHENTICITY

Magic mirror on the wall, who is the fairest one of all?[44]
—The Evil Queen in *Snow White*

I stepped into the hotel bathroom and flipped on the switch. Light flooded the tiny, white, sterile space. I'd been traveling all day. My makeup had worn off. My hair was a free-flowing, wind-blown mess. Exhausted, I bent over the sink and washed my hands. I grabbed the hand towel and glanced up into the mirror. I'm radiant. Holy cow and what the heck? Somehow, surprisingly, my skin tone is flawless. My cheeks are rosy. My eyes are sparkling, a brilliant emerald green hue with a dispersal of gold glitter. And my hair, oh my hair, is shiny and projecting a myriad of colorful hues of brown, gold, red, and blond. Even the gray that is growing and peeking out looks like beautiful, shimmery highlights.

For the love of all that is aged, what is this sorcery of magic lighting? I stood there, staring at myself, amazed. This has to be some kind of trick mirror. I stepped out of the bathroom and into the small sitting area where another mirror sat between the wet bar and the TV. Oh yes! There's the "me" I recognize. Ugh. I spied crow's feet, blotches of red and wind-burned cheeks and eyelids, the beginnings of—yep—a pimple, and wiry gray hairs sticking out at odd angles.

Did you ever watch the show, *Touched by an Angel*? The angels always appeared in normal human form until the end of the show, when they would reveal a message from God, as well as their supernatural identities. When the big reveal happened, the most glorious, flattering light would illuminate the characters as they spoke.

I swear the lighting engineer of *Touched by an Angel* designed this hotel bathroom. Let me tell you, I want to carry this heavenly light with me everywhere I go from now until I breathe my last breath. Seriously, I need answers, as well as a really big suitcase for this contraption. You want to see me? Sure thing, but I will need you to make room for my personal lighting thingy. I will never leave home without it.

The right lighting makes all the difference. Ask photographers. They schedule outdoor sessions at an exact time and location all because of the position of the sun and the type of light it casts, all so we can look our best. But think about it: do we hide away in our homes except during each day's golden hour? Of course not! So why is our standard for photos any different?

With the advent of smartphones, we can now manipulate lighting in photographs and change it with filter apps. We can look our best all the time with just the right tools. Until, of course, we see someone face-to-face or look at ourselves in a "non-angel-show" mirror; then, reality in all its unfiltered glory comes crashing through our façades. The use of all this technology has created a society increasingly bent toward vanity and image. We constantly obsess over the pictures of ourselves that we create and put out into the world, as if these manipulated images are more important than the real people we are underneath all the editing. We have become masterful at marketing our common lives to the masses. We spend hours trying to control others' perceptions of us. And to what end? We are, according to numerous studies tracking mental health and suicide rates, lonelier and more insecure than ever.

The following survey, released pre-Covid in May of 2018 by Cigna, already revealed alarming trends.[45] Cigna surveyed more than 20,000 U.S. adults, ages eighteen years and older:

- **Nearly half** of Americans report sometimes or always feeling alone (46 percent) or left out (47 percent).
- **Two in five** Americans sometimes or always feel that their relationships are not meaningful (43 percent) and that they are isolated from others (43 percent).
- **One in five** people report they rarely or never feel close to people (20 percent) or feel like there are people they can talk to (18 percent).
- **Only around half of Americans** (53 percent) have meaningful in-person social interactions, such as having an extended conversation with a friend or spending quality time with family, on a daily basis.
- **Generation Z (adults ages 18-22) is the loneliest generation** and claims to be in worse health than older generations, despite medical advancements.

This begs the obvious question: *why*? Perhaps we feel as if no one knows the "real us" anymore because we spend so much time polishing our fake images instead. Perhaps we are looking to digital "relationships" for validation and acceptance, instead of to our heavenly Father. In a world of fake beauty and superficial photo ops, it seems we've forgotten that nothing can cast us in a more favorable light than projecting the love of Jesus Christ to others. (That angel show definitely had that part right.)

I love the warm glow of a golden-hour photo shoot as much as the next gal, but let's not forget that such moments are brief glimpses into an entire lifespan of loving, learning, crying, and laughing. We absolutely must present our authentic selves to others if we want to have meaningful relationships with them.

> In a world of fake beauty and superficial photo ops, it seems we've forgotten that nothing can cast us in a more favorable light than projecting the love of Jesus Christ to others.

Charm is deceptive, and beauty is fleeting;
but a woman who fears the LORD is to be praised.
(Prov. 31:30)

Your beauty should not come from outward adornment, such as elaborate hairstyles and the wearing of gold jewelry or fine clothes. Rather, it should be that of your inner self, the unfading beauty of a gentle and quiet spirit, which is of great worth in God's sight.
(1 Pet. 3:3–4)

God doesn't want us to hide away and only put our "best face forward." He wants us to spend time with Him and come away with radiant faces like Moses (Exod. 34), eager to share with others what the Lord has said and done.

I took a walk recently while listening to praise and worship music as the sun shone brightly behind me, warming my back. I rank five-foot-nothing on the height chart, so I noticed the particularly tall shadow with long legs projected in front of me. I snapped a picture and posted it on social media stating, "I'm always tallest when I'm standing in the *Son*shine."

The right lighting does make a difference. We chastise the Evil Queen for being so openly obsessed with her own vanity, but isn't there a part of her in us all, wondering how we measure up and how others see us? I think God would love to tell us to stop all our striving and just be real with one another, to show everyone our authentic selves, and to focus on the Light of the World more than we focus on the lighting of our filter apps and vanity mirrors.

Let's step into the *Son*light, where everyone is a beautiful child of God. Let's allow His character and beauty to shine through us all.

Hope

*Not only so, but we also glory in our
sufferings, because we know that suffering
produces perseverance; perseverance,
character; and character, hope.*
(Rom. 5:3–4)

FACING HOPE

*May the God of hope fill you with all joy and
peace as you trust in him, so that you may overflow
with hope by the power of the Holy Spirit.
(Rom. 15:13)*

W hen Moses spent time with God on the mountaintop,
he returned with a radiant face. He covered his face
with a veil because the Israelites couldn't handle seeing
it. Jesus forever lifted that veil of separation between
God and us, His followers. If Moses's face shone with
the glory of God, how much more will ours when we, too,
spend time with our heavenly Father and His son, Jesus?

*Now if the ministry that brought death, which was engraved
in letters on stone, came with glory, so that the Israelites
could not look steadily at the face of Moses because of its
glory, transitory though it was, will not the ministry of the
Spirit be even more glorious? If the ministry that brought
condemnation was glorious, how much more glorious is the
ministry that brings righteousness! For what was glorious
has no glory now in comparison with the surpassing glory.
And if what was transitory came with glory, how much
greater is the glory of that which lasts! Therefore, since
we have such a hope, we are very bold. ... Now the Lord*

is the Spirit, and where the Spirit of the Lord is, there is freedom. And we all, who with unveiled faces contemplate the Lord's glory, are being transformed into his image with ever-increasing glory, which comes from the Lord, who is the Spirit.
(2 Cor. 3:7–12, 17–18)

When we have suffered, persevered, and developed character through our life experiences, we are raw and ripe for the grace and mercy found in Jesus Christ. He is our hope. Jesus is our help in our present and future times of need, as well as our hope of salvation and glory to come. When we fully comprehend the depth of this grace, we find ourselves completely in love with Him, our faces radiant, and we are ready and willing to serve Him in anything He asks of us.

Dear God,
You have given us our only hope: Jesus Christ. Our salvation is free, but it cost You everything. As we embrace Your priceless gift, help us to bear witness to Your love and mercy so others can come to know You. It's all that matters, Lord. May we bask in Your grace as we turn to our Rock, Redeemer, and Friend so our lives may mirror that of Your precious son, Jesus, our eternal hope.
Amen

Additional verses to read about hope:

Hebrews 10:23–25
John 14:1–14
Romans 5:5
Colossians 1:27
Jeremiah 29:11
Isaiah 40:30–31
Psalm 71:5
Psalm 130:5
Psalm 119:81
Psalm 147:11
Proverbs 10:28

FACING SPIRITUAL GIFTS

Just be yourself; there is no one better.[46]
—Taylor Swift

I was completely envious of my child. It was Thanksgiving break, and while I stood in the kitchen washing dishes, planning menus, and making grocery lists, I looked out the back window and saw my son standing in the middle of the backyard in nothing but his underwear. He was blowing loudly and constantly on a whistle. I spied a stick shoved in the waistband of his undies, a dollar store jump rope hanging around his neck, and a toy bow and arrow in his non-whistle-yielding hand. I shook my head, laughed to myself, and just stood there watching him play in a world of his own creating, carefree, and fully confident in himself and his abilities to save the day from turmoil.

This boy of mine is quite a study in oxymorons. He is completely confident, yet anxious. He is friendly, but doesn't want to be in the spotlight. He is intelligent and yet struggles with test-taking. He is impulsive, but always deep in thought. He is messy, and yet loves to collect and organize things. He is deeply affectionate, yet prone to anger. My son is truly an original, and I love catching glimpses of the inner workings of his mind while he plays.

Do we remember how it felt to be playing like my son was on Thanksgiving break? Completely unaware of how we looked, what others might think, and whether or not we were doing it "right"?

As I have grown older, I have returned to many of the things I loved to do as a child. I discovered that many of the activities I put away in favor of "adulting" actually bring me the most joy and fulfillment, regardless of my age. If we want to truly unearth the giftings God has placed within us, we have to stop trying to be all the things that we aren't, and instead just be all that we are— the people He created us to be from the very beginning.

All three of my children are so completely different from one another, but they all grew up in the same house with the same parents. You could not catch my youngest child leading worship for all the money in the world, but it feeds my oldest child's soul in ways nothing else can. My middle child loves to express herself through sketching and painting, but I'm incapable of drawing a stick figure proportionately.

God created the universe with an endless array of beautiful attributes, and we humans are just a tiny fraction of it. The Bible in Genesis says mankind is "created in His own image," so we are a reflection of God Himself. The world misses out on the full picture of God's character when we stifle the unique ways in which He has created each one of us.

> *Each of you should use whatever gift you*
> *have received to serve others, as faithful stewards*
> *of God's grace in its various forms.*
> *(1 Pet. 4:10)*

Our cumulative gifts paint a picture of the fullness of God's grace, mercy, and creativity. Your gifts, your voice, and your perspective are all uniquely created by God to reach someone else for the sake of His kingdom. We like to think our talents, interests, and hobbies are for our own benefit and enjoyment, but those are the very God-given gifts He wants to use to reach others for His purposes. When we participate in something that leaves us feeling full, inspired, joyful, and energetic—*this* is operating inside our God-given gifts. This is also how we collectively reflect the diverse character of God.

> Your gifts, your voice, and your perspective are all uniquely created by God to reach someone else for the sake of His kingdom.

There are different kinds of gifts, but the same Spirit distributes them. There are different kinds of service, but the same Lord. There are different kinds of working, but in all of them and in everyone it is the same God at work.
(1 Cor. 12:4–6)

Have you ever signed up for a job or volunteer duty that absolutely zapped your energy? After one or two appointments with this calendar date, did you start dreading the next one? Did it start to feel like an obligation instead of a choice or opportunity? These are tell-tale signs that you are operating *outside* of your gifts. When we busy ourselves with things God hasn't ordained for us, we can miss the wonderful things He planned for us in the first place. No one can do it all. And every bit of time we spend on something God hasn't planned for us is a moment of time that hasn't been spent working toward the fulfillment of His ultimate plan for our lives.

Coming into our spiritual gifts means we have to let go of all the things we *aren't*, so we can celebrate all the things we innately *are*. We are told as children, "You can be anything you want to be!" I believe that's a fallacy. We can, however, be anything and everything *God* wants us to be. God has a divine purpose outlined for each one of us, a way for us to join in His work here on earth in our own unique ways. Our gifts match those callings. No one can do the job that He created you for, but you. He designed each of us with specific works in mind.

Coming into our spiritual gifts means we have to let go of all the things we *aren't*, so we can celebrate all the things we innately *are*.

For just as each of us has one body with many members, and these members do not all have the same function, so in Christ we, though many, form one body, and each member belongs to all the others. We have different gifts, according to the grace given to each of us.
(Rom. 12:4–6a)

We create the magnificent tapestry of the world when we collaborate with our gifts. The good news? Romans 11:29 says God's gifts and His calling upon our lives are irrevocable. So the "you" that God created you to be, can never be snatched away. Spend some time today thinking about the things you really love to do. These activities should come naturally, and they should energize you and bring you joy. Pray for God to show you how to use those unique parts of yourself for His kingdom and His glory.

Ask for the specific ways God wants you to reflect His character and grace. And then, may you go about that work with the confidence of a preschooler standing in the backyard in his underwear, saving the world.

FACING IDENTITY

It's really easy to fall into the trap of believing that what we do is more important than what we are. Of course, it's the opposite that's true: What we are ultimately determines what we do.[47]
—Mister Rogers

At the ripe old age of seven, my son knew exactly what he wanted to be when he grew up.

"Mommy," he said, "when I grow up, I want to be a homeless dad. You know, a dad that stays home and takes care of the kids. Because they might want me to be home with them. My wife can go to work. She'll be a principal at the school just for our kids because we're going to have 100 kids! I will drive our school bus. But I will not change diapers. I'm going to be a scientist at home too, and I will build a robot that looks like me that changes the diapers."

It was a mouthful. And a life-full, to say the least.

We make a habit of asking kids what they want to be when they grow up. I think it's partially because we love to hear their limitless dreams, but I also believe it's because we have a need to put labels and identities on one another. We feel if we can just slap the right label on those around us, suddenly everyone will "make sense." Watch any movie that centers around the junior high or high school years, and you can see this penchant in action. Words like jock, prep, nerd, goth, and brain not-so-accurately pin identity on others like a nametag. Ever notice how the storylines in these movies always revolve around one or more characters breaking out of the stereotypes to which they've been assigned, as they learn how to embrace who they truly are, though?

We like to think that as adults we are too mature to participate in this rampant identity-pinning, but we're not. The labels change, but the practice remains. As adults, we use relationship status, employment status, hobbies, and more to try to better understand and categorize those around us. If you needed to introduce yourself to a complete stranger in one minute, what would you say? Probably something along the lines of: My name is Nicki Carlson. I've been married to a wonderful man named John for more than twenty-five years. We have three children, ages twenty, seventeen, and thirteen. I am a stay-at-home mom and a writer. My hobbies include singing, playing tennis, playing piano, reading, and gardening.

Nothing wrong with that, right? But is this who I really am? Is this my identity?

Society has taught us that identity is what we do, but that's not the true meaning behind our identities. Dictionary.com lists the following as one of the definitions of identity: "a condition or character as to who a person or what a thing is; the qualities, beliefs, etc., that distinguish or identify a person or thing." Nowhere in that definition does it speak to what a person *does*, only what a person *is* and what a person *believes*.

So what is my identity? Child of God and follower of Jesus Christ. Everything else, as we say here in the south, is just icing on the cake. We can do a great many things in this life—many of them admirable, like mothering, teaching, serving others, and fighting against injustice—but none of them will compare to our decision to claim our inheritance in Jesus Christ.

But you are a chosen people, a royal priesthood, a holy nation, God's special possession, that you may declare the praises of him who called you out of darkness into his wonderful light.
(1 Pet. 2:9)

But whoever is united with the Lord is one with him in spirit.
(1 Cor. 6:17)

When we fail to root our identity in Christ, all our labors are in vain, and in many cases, outright idolatry.

Take motherhood, for example. If our identity lies in our ability to mother, what happens if our children die? What happens if our children stray from the path we set before them? What happens if they disown us? What if I tie my own self-worth to the "successes" of my child and then she feels so much pressure to perform that she hates her life and never feels she is measuring up to my expectations? If we tie our identity to our job, what happens if we are let go due to downsizing? What happens if we make a mistake that leads to job termination?

By contrast, when we base our identity in Christ, He brings a kingdom perspective to our lives, our missions, and our activities. As a mother, for example, my home can be filled with the same unconditional grace, love, and mercy that God offers me, instead of expectations and condemnation. As a professional, my self-worth is not determined by my current job situation.

Our identities are not tied to our circumstances; they are tied

> Our identities are not tied to our circumstances; they are tied to our Savior.

to our Savior. If we want to know *who* we are, we must first know *whose* we are.

> *Yet to all who did receive him, to those who believed in his name, he gave the right to become children of God.*
> (John 1:12)

The more we get to know the character of God by spending time in prayer and in His Word, the more we become like Him, and the more our image and identity become indistinguishable from His.

> *And we all, who with unveiled faces*
> *contemplate the Lord's glory, are being transformed*
> *into his image with ever-increasing glory, which*
> *comes from the Lord, who is the Spirit.*
> (2 Cor. 3:18)

I remember reading a question one time that stopped me dead in my tracks: If a foreign or domestic agency assigned to round up all the followers of Jesus came to your door, would they find enough evidence to take you and your family away and convict you? To put it another way, are you living out your identity in Christ? Or, are you presenting yourself to the world according to your circumstances, instead of your Savior? God gives us abilities and blessings in abundance, but none is more important than the gift of salvation in Jesus Christ. When we deeply anchor our very identity to our Savior, the stormy circumstances of the world will not throw us off-course.

Whether you have a hundred children or none, are single or married to a principal, work in an office or at home building diaper-changing robots, know that you are deeply loved and valued by the God of the universe. You are His. It's who you are.

FACING WORSHIP

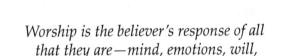

Worship is the believer's response of all
that they are—mind, emotions, will,
body—to what God is and says and does.[48]
—Warren W. Wiersbe

I struggle terribly with migraines. I faced a time in my life before diagnosis in which I was basically home-bound for months. I couldn't drive, and social environments with fluorescent lighting and noise was more than I could tolerate. I underwent tests, procedures, and scans to rule out everything, including but not limited to lupus, meningitis, rheumatoid arthritis, heart disorders, and multiple sclerosis. It was a very scary time. I did extensive physical therapy for over a year to correct herniated discs in my neck that were contributing pinched nerve pain to the debilitating migraines. I landed in the emergency room on numerous occasions, unable to control or withstand the dizziness and pounding in my head without emergency intervention.

I say these things not to elicit sympathy, but to let you know that I do know suffering and pain. The most difficult part of this time in my life? Not being able to care for my family in the ways I wanted to, and not being able to worship in song. You see, I've spent my entire life singing. I served as a worship leader for years, and for over a year I couldn't sing without triggering a migraine. To this day, no one is exactly sure what the connection was, whether it was a response to the muscles in the face, neck, and shoulders tightening when I sang, or if it was something more spiritual in nature. But I couldn't sing at all, and it just about broke my heart.

I distinctly remember determinedly going to church one Sunday and sitting during the praise songs until I was compelled to rise to my feet, and even though a single note could not escape from my throat, my heart and soul were praising God with every ounce of life in them. Tears streamed down my cheeks as I worshiped my God and Creator in silence. Words often fall short as an offering to a perfect, holy, omnipotent, and eternal God, anyway. I am so thankful that He hears the cries of our hearts. I praised God that morning for who He is, for the blessing of community, and for the intimacy of fellowship with other believers.

> The righteous cry out, and the Lord hears them;
> he delivers them from all their troubles.
> (Ps. 34:17)

Worship is a beautiful expression of shared experience, connection, and praise. As worship pastor Darlene Zschech says, it is a "declaration, a victory cry, proclaiming faith to stand firm in the place God has given you." [49]

I learned during this difficult period of my life that worship can take many forms, and that my need to exalt the name of my God and Savior could and would overpower any disability my body might encounter. I felt as if I embodied the rocks in the following verse:

When he came near the place where the road goes down the Mount of Olives, the whole crowd of disciples began joyfully to praise God in loud voices for all the miracles they had seen … Some of the Pharisees in the crowd said to Jesus, "Teacher, rebuke your disciples!" Jesus replied, "I tell you, if they keep quiet, the stones will cry out."
(Luke 19:37, 39-40)

I accepted I might never vocally lead worship again, but that did not mean I wouldn't continue to worship. When we worship and offer praise, we stop focusing on ourselves and turn to seek God's face. Our perspective shifts from asking to offering, from temporary matters to eternal ones, and from momentary suffering to eternal glory. Worshiping God isn't about us; it's all about Him.

Worshiping God isn't about us; it's all about Him.

I also learned during this period in my life to employ the name of Jesus Christ to protect me during worship so that He might work through me to accomplish His plans. During guided prayer with a very special woman, I had a vision of Jesus standing directly behind me while I was vocally leading worship. My savior held His arms stretched around me to my front. He was a circle of protection against any attack that might come upon me. I became an open conduit for the Holy Spirit rising up within me, flowing out through my mouth and into the room. Within a few weeks of this vision, and through a great deal of prayer, I slowly began venturing into worship leadership again, and I now lead frequently and without migraines.

My very eloquent Christian brother, Spencer Thomas, has taught me a great deal about worship. When I asked him to explain worship in just a few sentences, he said this: "To worship is to apply an ever-increasing amount of worth onto something. Offering your life as a living sacrifice is the ultimate worship, because worth is determined by a price that is willing to be paid. And no greater price has ever been paid than Jesus giving his life for ours."

When I was in the midst of my valley of suffering, I wrote the following in my journal one day:

My purpose here is to praise His name. To cry out with all that is in me to my heavenly Father. If my voice is silenced, then I will dance. If I cannot dance, then I will smile and embrace. If I cannot embrace, then my very spirit will sing out to Him, and He will hear me.
I am not me—I am incomplete—if His name is not on my lips. The battle has already been won. My suffering is but temporary. The serpent has been crushed under the heel of my Savior. My Savior. And I will sing of the victory and the celebration and the glory that He is forever due. Through His grace, my worship might bring others nearer to Him. (Father, if it please you, may it be so.) Through His benevolence, I may feel joy in the offering. Through His great love, I may feel Him near.
But if I do not, I will still worship.
Because it is what I was created to do.

Worship was never meant to be only something we do in church on Sunday mornings. Worship leader and Christian songwriter Graham Kendrick says, "Worship is at heart a person offered to God, claiming no rights, making no more selfish demands than a dead man does, but living fully, richly and wholly to God and by His power."[50]

Our greatest act of worship? Turn to God. Fix our hearts and minds on Him. And live our lives fully surrendered to the authority of Jesus Christ.

FACING ATTENTION

"Turn down your music!"
"What?"
"Turn down your music!"
"Whaaat?!"
"TURN DOWN YOUR MUSIC! IT'S TOO LOUD!"
—every mother and child, ever

My newly-turned-sixteen-year-old daughter sat beside me in the passenger seat while I drove her to school in the darkness of early morning. She exudes joy regardless of the time of day, while I am decidedly not a morning person. My girl loves nothing more than riding in a car, windows all the way down with wind blowing her long hair, singing at the top of her lungs to the latest pop song. In a rare moment when she's not bubbly, an upbeat song will instantly transform her mood.

This particular morning, she sweetly asked, "Mom, can we listen to some music?" I answered, "Of course! You pick," and instantly the sounds of an angst-ridden, yet sassy twenty-something-girl completely flooded the vehicle's interior. All of ten seconds later, she dove into a story about a class project she'd been working on and how she was feeling about it, and I instinctively turned the volume down so I could hear her better. A disappointed glance escaped her face before she could prevent it, but she continued talking to me. I knew she wanted to listen to music, but I wanted to hear every word she was sharing with me. I didn't want to be distracted.

Have you ever stopped to think about how God listens to us? Or how we listen to Him? Scripture says He hears us.

The LORD is far from the wicked, but he hears
the prayer of the righteous.
(Prov. 15:29)

The righteous cry out, and the LORD hears them;
he delivers them from all their troubles.
(Ps. 34:17)

In addition to hearing us, God's word also says that He responds.

You, LORD, hear the desire of the afflicted;
you encourage them, and you listen to their cry.
(Ps. 10:17)

Have you considered your posture as you listen to God? Do you intentionally turn down all the noise around you so you can hang on His every word, as I did in the car with my daughter? Do you free your hands from distractions, or place a pen and sheet of paper nearby so you can remember His words? Do you give Him your full attention?

Assemble the people—men, women and children,
and the foreigners residing in your towns—so they
can listen and learn to fear the LORD your God and follow
carefully all the words of this law.
(Deut. 31:12)

Do not forget the jealousy of our God. He doesn't want to share your affection and attention with other things. That's numero uno in the Ten Commandments, after all.

You shall have no other gods before me.
(Exod. 20:3)

I said to you, "I am the Lord your God; do
not worship the gods of the Amorites, in whose land you
live." But you have not listened to me.
(Judg. 6:10)

When we enter into quiet time, prayer, or study time with the Lord, we are entering a sacred space with the God of the universe. Turn off the TV. Silence your phone. Quiet your mind. Get still. Slow your breathing. Give Him all the attention He is due. God could not care less where we seek Him, only that we do seek Him.

My daughter probably hears God best with Christian music playing in the background. I prefer silence or the sound of flowing water, so I do some of my best listening in the shower. Some of my closest friends feel nearest to God and hear Him most clearly when surrounded by nature. When we posture ourselves as attentive listeners, we become fertile soil for God. All that He says becomes planted like a seed in the healthy soil of our hearts and minds, ready to burst forth in blooms at His designated time.

Stop for a moment and think about this: Can you imagine the heartbreak of knowing God Almighty had a message specifically for you, but you were too busy or distracted to hear it? To know that you missed His words for you? This very thing happened time and time again with God's people in the Bible. The Lord's people either didn't hear, heard but did not listen, or listened but did not obey. How many times did the prophets of the Old Testament begin their prophecies and pronouncements with the single word "listen"? These messages came from God Himself, and He began by telling His children to sit up straight, stop fiddling with stuff, and listen. We are such children.

While you were doing all these things, declares the LORD,
I spoke to you again and again, but you did not listen;
I called you, but you did not answer.
(Jer. 7:13)

God wants our full attention. Not because *He* needs it, but because *we* need it. He desires an intimate relationship with us. He wants to involve us in the work of His kingdom for our own sake, not for His. And unlike our own words, God's message remains perfect and eternal.

> God wants our full attention. Not because *He* needs it, but because *we* need it.

The grass withers and the flowers fall,
but the word of our God endures forever.
(Isa. 40:8)

Have you ever held a sick and hurting child and been incapable of making them well or even comforting them? Have you ever watched a friend suffer a broken heart and imploding life and been unable to mend it? Have you sat with a loved one languishing in grief and failed at making them feel better? We place God in this position when we fail to be in relationship with Him. God stands ready, willing, and able to help us with all these things and more, if we would just stop and listen to all He wants to say to us. Do not ignore Him. His heart's desire is for us to draw near to Him and learn all we can about His character and His ways. We can't do that with divided attention. Let Him instruct you. Be fertile soil for the Lord. Turn down the radio and turn your face toward your heavenly Father. Listen. Be intentional about giving Him your attention because, trust me, you don't want to miss a word.

Facing Discipleship

Our Lord's conception of discipleship is not that we work for God, but that God works through us.[51]
—Oswald Chambers

Today is one of those "It's good to be a mom" days. We moms like to grab these days when they come around and, like Mary in the Bible, hold them close, pondering them in our hearts. I've heard other moms say they tuck a moment like this in their pocket and keep it for a rainy day.

In my town, we combine four public elementary schools at the sixth-grade level, and we dump all those little weirdos on one campus by themselves. This ensures that every kid is on a new campus, surrounded by a lot of new faces, with all of them doing a lot of new things like changing clothes for athletics and hauling around a heavy band instrument for the first time. It's slightly managed chaos at best. My youngest is on this sixth-grade campus this year. Today, near the beginning of the second month of school, I entered the building to deliver some medication my son forgot to take that morning. I arrived in the middle of—*oh the horror*—lunchtime. I followed the raucous noise to the cafeteria where my eyes searched for my precious darling. About the same time that I spotted him, a friend of his caught sight of me and proceeded to poke my son and point at me, and I smiled and just motioned for my son to head my direction.

Now, hear me out. I don't know one single solitary parent that is truly comfortable imposing themselves on their tween's tribe in the middle of their sacred lunchtime on their own school turf. I at least know that I myself have no clue how to behave in such situations. It's like trying to feed a pet lion. Will they want to play? Will they let you pet them? Will they act sweet and then turn and suddenly bite the hand that feeds them? One never knows.

Trying to be as invisible as possible to avoid embarrassing my kid, I ducked behind a wall. He joined me there behind the visual barricade, and I explained he forgot take his medicine and proceeded to give it to him. He thanked me, and I asked a couple of quick questions, which he surprisingly answered with very little annoyance in his voice. Not wanting to overstay my welcome, I then said, "Okay, bud, I'll see you later," and walked back out from behind the wall and into view. He turned to walk away and then stopped, turned back to me, and said, "Wait! I need a mommy hug."

And then this twelve-year-old boy walked over to me and gave me a full-frontal hug in front of God and the entire school.

I was momentarily speechless.

But I tried to play it cool and simply said, "See you later," and turned my back on the cafeteria, hiding my gigantic smile and the little tear in my eye. In the one shining moment, I actually thought to myself, "I must be doing something right."

For the purposes of this chapter, we will call parenting what it is: discipling. But you don't have to be a parent to disciple others. I've spent a great deal of time with middle-school-aged kids in small groups, Bible studies, youth group activities, and in my home. A lot of people think I'm crazy for it, but I love those little adolescent freaks. Tweens and young teens—more than any other age group I know—desperately seek love and acceptance. Their need for validation drives almost every single decision they make. If we can introduce the love and acceptance of God to this age group, and if we can help them cultivate a relationship with Christ, so much of their lives will fall into place.

Discipleship doesn't have to be an organized activity like the examples above, though. All discipleship or mentoring requires is investing time and attention on others. It might look like a weekly phone call to an elderly person, a conversation with your child's friend at the breakfast table after a sleepover, or a chat over coffee with your next-door neighbor. I learned a long time ago that I was not the kind of person to go on mission trips to far-away places where I would need to "rough it" or testify about the Good News with strangers on the street. God just didn't build me that way.

God did, however, give me a heart for relational ministry. For adoption. For loving on kids that aren't living in my home, but who might spend a night here once in a while. He gave me a desire to write and to teach, and so I use those gifts to share with others what God has done in my own life. I may not be skilled at telling a homeless stranger on the street or someone who speaks a different language than me that Jesus loves them, but I will sing it or play it with my team during worship, and I will tell my daughter's friend over coffee on Saturday morning, and I will write about it until I run out of words.

Discipleship doesn't have to be complicated. Just look back at your own life and identify the ways God has been there for you, rescued you, saved you, and loved you; then, ask Him to show you opportunities to share those personal experiences with others. His heart is for His children, so He will always honor that prayer.

Discipleship may look like a one-on-one conversation with a close friend while sitting at Starbucks, or teaching a small group Bible study, or delivering a devotional speech to a huge roomful of strangers. It's different for everyone. The possibilities are endless, because God's creativity in reaching us is endless. The point is, He will lead you according to the gifts He has already given you, so you have no reason to fear. And praise be to God that He sent a Helper to guide us with this task—the Holy Spirit!

But you will receive power when the Holy Spirit comes on you; and you will be my witnesses in Jerusalem, and in all Judea and Samaria, and to the ends of the earth.
Acts 1:8

Do not hide from the world all that God has done and is doing for you. Follow the Holy Spirit's leading and share God's story of your life with others.

With the power and guidance of His Spirit within us, we can disciple others and bear witness to God's saving love and grace. Do not hide from the world all that God has done and is doing for you. Follow the Holy Spirit's leading and share God's story of your life with others. He is faithful to help us carry out this mission.

In all my prayers for all of you, I always pray with joy because of your partnership in the gospel from the first day until now, being confident of this, that he

who began a good work in you will carry it on to completion
until the day of Christ Jesus.
(Phil. 1:4-6)

As my friend Josh Smithson, a YoungLife director, says, we "earn the right to be heard" when we first enter into relationship with someone. Be a friend first. Or a parent. Or a volunteer. Or a neighbor. God will open the door for you to testify when the time is right. Until then, live a life worthy of Christ, a life capable of pointing others to Him simply by example.

Deep down inside, we're all still awkward sixth-graders desperate for love and acceptance. Be the person someone else will remember for offering him or her eternal validation in Christ. There's no greater fulfillment in this world than bringing another person to the arms of Jesus. It's even better than a Mommy hug in front of the whole school.

FACING CONTENTMENT

Nothing is enough for the man to whom enough is too little.[52]
—Max Lucado

School starts in two days, so I am firmly entrenched in my usual back-to-school funk. I know a lot of moms count down the days until their precious darlings go back to school, but that's typically not me. I'm more apt to say and think things like, "Did he read enough over the summer? Did she practice her instrument well? Is he brain-dead from all the video games I allowed him to play? Did she see her friends enough or will it be awkward when they see each other? Will he remember his manners?" After the anxiety, I can usually be found rocking myself in a corner, sucking my thumb with tears streaming down my face, asking questions like, "Where has the time gone? I just want it to be summer forever so we can all be together all the live-long day! What has happened to my *babies*?!"

Nobody ever describes me as "simple," and I can't imagine why. Perhaps it's because my heart is permanently attached to my sleeve, for all the world to see. My husband is a tear-stained-shirt-wearing saint, but don't tell him I said that.

It never fails that just as I begin to bemoan my precious angels leaving the safety of my nest, a scene like this also takes place:

Cue sing-song voice from the backseat of a car in 100-degree Texas summer heat where the ice cream is melting on the way home from the grocery store

"Mommyyyy is meannnn. She won't let me have my Spriiiiite. I am not happy at her anymore. I don't want to live with her. I'm going to Houston to live!"

End scene

So, amidst the growing up, the milestones, the days that crawl by and the years that fly by, there's this thing happening called *life*. And if you're anything like me, you ask yourself the "enough" questions in the midst of said life. Did I read my Bible enough? Did I tell my family members often enough that I love them? Was I available enough for my friends and others in need? Did I work enough, laugh enough, play enough, create enough, listen enough, and speak enough?

Somewhere between *not enough* and *too much*, there is a place I call *contentment*. For a reformed perfectionist like myself, it can be difficult to locate. Charles Spurgeon said, "You say, 'If I had a little more, I should be very satisfied.' You make a mistake. If you are not content with what you have, you would not be satisfied if it were doubled."[53]

We waste our time when we long for the "next best thing" because with God, the *next* thing is never the *final* thing. God always has more in store for us. Likewise, if we spend our days constantly looking ahead to the next phase or acquisition, we miss the joy and beauty of today's gifts. That's why, after all, we call today the "present." Situational contentment lies in learning to appreciate the good gifts He has given us *today*, and in turning our hearts and faces toward Him each and every day of our lives.

But godliness with contentment is great gain. For we brought
nothing into the world, and we can take nothing out of it.
(1 Tim. 6:6–7)

Beyond situational contentment, we can strive for spiritual contentment. Paul explains this in his letter to the Philippians:

I am not saying this because I am in need, for I have learned
to be content whatever the circumstances. I know what it is
to be in need, and I know what it is to have plenty. I have
learned the secret of being content in any and every situation,
whether well fed or hungry, whether living in plenty or in
want. I can do all this through him who gives me strength.
(Phil. 4:11–13)

We cannot be content doing less than what God asks of us; similarly, we cannot be content trying to do an ever-increasing amount of "more."

Christ is the key to our contentment. In his book *Cure for the Common Life*, author Max Lucado describes the place of contentment as the intersection of our abilities and affections. It's like the sweet spot of life. Lucado says, "Look back over your life. What have you consistently done well? What have you loved to do? Stand at the intersection of your affections and successes and find your uniqueness."[54] Lucado goes on to say that we cannot be just *anything* we want to be, but we can in fact be *everything* that God wants us to be, through a relationship with His son Jesus Christ.

I saw a meme recently that read, "Someone, somewhere, is depending on you to do what God has called you to do." Not every*one*. Not every*thing*. Just what you have been *called* to do. We cannot be content doing less than what God asks of us; similarly, we cannot be content trying to do an ever-increasing amount of "more." True contentment comes through intimately knowing Christ and seeking to serve only Him.

The fear of the LORD *leads to life;*
then one rests content, untouched by trouble.
(Prov. 19:23)

Spiritual contentment is often described as peace. It's an attitude or state of mind in which a believer can transcend one's circumstances to find joy and satisfaction in simply experiencing the presence of God and serving Him in all things. Again, we can look to the letter Paul wrote to the Philippians, while he was jailed, for inspiration.

I eagerly expect and hope that I will in no way be ashamed,
but will have sufficient courage so that now as always
Christ will be exalted in my body, whether by life or by death.
For to me, to live is Christ and to die is gain.
(Phil. 1:20–21)

Contentment isn't waiting at the pinnacle of some mountain or completion of a far-off dream. Contentment is our companion every step we take on the path God has laid out for us. It's in the small decisions like leaving work in time to make our kid's soccer game, and in the big decisions like choosing which job offer to take. It's communion and fellowship with Him along the journey of discovering the treasures He has stored inside of us to share with the world—those pieces of ourselves that are a reflection of Him.

Whether we are in want or plenty, just beginning our story or near the end, we can find contentment in the love, grace, and mercy of Jesus Christ and by walking through all our days in relationship with and service to Him.

FACING OTHERS

I know of only one duty,
And that is to love.[55]
—Albert Camus

W hile driving in the car one day, my son volunteered some random, unprompted information. He said, "Sometimes, I like to stick my tongue out at the clouds, Mommy."

I said, "You do?"

He replied, "Yes," followed by a long pause. "But not the white ones. Only the gray ones."

I was baffled by his pointless cloud racism, as well as his need to tongue-flip-them-off. It made me wonder why, as humans, we selectively choose subjects upon which we unload animosity and truly evil behavior.

Love does no harm to a neighbor.
Therefore love is the fulfillment of the law.
(Rom. 13:10)

As I ponder this good word from the Bible, I'm finding that simply "doing no harm" is no longer enough. Doing no harm means doing nothing. Doing nothing maintains the status quo. And in an established society with historic and systemic injustices, the status quo is anything but "unharmful." Just ask a homosexual or a person of color.

Jesus did everything he could to break up the status quo. He routinely challenged the rules and practices of those in authority. He broke bread with the outcasts, hung out with sinners, and taught the message of God when, where, and to whom He was specifically told not to do so. He spoke up for the downtrodden, the mistake-makers, and the societal insignificants—the "others."

We like to believe we're those people, too, but most of us are not. Do we sin? Of course. But most of us also fall into the status of the majority: Educated. Employed. White. Religious. Middle to upper-middle class. Heterosexual. Positions of authority. We probably don't even realize it, but we are part of the "In" group. The "It" crowd. The "Haves."

In other words, we're the Pharisees.

In Jesus's time, the Pharisees were known for their adherence to liturgy, rules, and ritual. They prided themselves on being members of their own "church club." They often tested Jesus by trying to catch him contradicting or refuting Judaic law, and thereby in their minds, proving He was not the promised Messiah.

> *Hearing that Jesus had silenced the Sadducees,*
> *the Pharisees got together. One of them, an expert in*
> *the law, tested him with this question: "Teacher, which is*
> *the greatest commandment in the Law?" Jesus replied:*
> *"Love the Lord your God with all your heart and with all*
> *your soul and with all your mind. This is the first and*
> *greatest commandment. And the second is like it: Love your*
> *neighbor as yourself. All the Law and the Prophets hang on*
> *these two commandments."*
> *(Matt. 22:34–40)*

This passage is what we call the Greatest Commandments. I want to focus on the second half, "loving our neighbors as ourselves." Let's look to Jesus once again for insight into how this should look.

When Jesus was ready to begin His ministry here on earth, did He go to the synagogue and gather the chief priests? Did He seek out the most well-known scholars of the Torah? Did He align Himself with the governmental rulers and authorities? Did He stand on a mountaintop and shout to the masses that He was the Messiah, and that all should turn from their wicked ways and immediately bow down to Him or risk eternal damnation in the fiery pits of hell? No. The first thing Jesus did was gather up some neighbors we now like to call the twelve disciples.

With His disciples and countless others, Jesus ministered time and again through personal relationships with people. Not just *certain* people, but literally *any person* with whom He came into contact. He spoke one-on-one, through stories about situations common to His listeners, and reassured them—always, always reassured them—of God's great eternal love for them.

Dear friends, let us love one another, for love comes from God. Everyone who loves has been born of God and knows God. Whoever does not love does not know God, because God is love. This is how God showed his love among us: He sent his one and only Son into the world that we might live through him. This is love: not that we loved God, but that he loved us and sent his Son as an atoning sacrifice for our sins. Dear friends, since God so loved us, we also ought to love one another.
(1 John 4:7–11)

Before we can attempt to love others, we must first seek the one who created love and is the embodiment of love. It stands to reason that if God is love, then the best example of it we'll ever see was walking the earth thousands of years ago and went by the name of Jesus.

Before we can attempt to love others, we must first seek the one who created love and is the embodiment of love.

Because God went to the painful extreme of sending His son Jesus to die here on earth, we should pay really close attention to what He did and how He acted when He was here. That seems obvious, but I think we feel good about ourselves for going to our air-conditioned churches with coffee and donuts and comfortable seats, when if Jesus were here on the earth again, that's probably the last place we would find Him. It's certainly not where the people in Jesus's time found Him. I think we would find Jesus today ministering in the streets, assisting the poor, feeding the hungry, caring for the orphans and homeless, rescuing the sex workers, and giving help and hope to the addicted. You know— the ones we Christians tend to shy away from. Now don't get me wrong. I believe churches are crucial to society and to Christianity, but being a Jesus-follower doesn't stop with church attendance. Jesus taught us that loving others involves relationships, and we can't do relational ministry from the safety of our pews.

If we're having trouble loving our neighbors (and rest assured, if they're human beings, they're our neighbors), we need to draw near to the author and embodiment of love itself. Only through the example of God's sacrificial love through Jesus Christ can we understand the depth and quality of His love for us, and then through the in-dwelling of the Holy Spirit, we can also receive the ability to love our neighbors in the same way that He loves us.

FACING VICTORY

Nothing paralyzes our lives like the attitude that things can never change. We need to remind ourselves that God can change things. Outlook determines outcome. If we see only the problems, we will be defeated; but if we see the possibilities in the problems, we can have victory.[56]
—Warren Wiersbe

"Mrs. Carlson, your son may never walk. He should be crawling by now. There is still considerable stiffness in his right leg. I'm afraid we are going to have to label him as developmentally delayed." The words from the physical therapist landed like a lead brick. My precious baby boy, nine months old, just received a frightening prognosis. The therapist continued to speak encouragement and hope, but the words "may never walk" and "developmentally delayed" kept playing in a loop in my brain.

I thought we were past these kinds of nightmare appointments. After all, we heard "Your son may never tolerate solid food" from the gastroenterologist, and we proved him wrong. We also heard "Your son may have Crohn's disease, or Hirschsprung disease, or lupus, or cerebral palsy." Also wrong. So I refused to believe this therapist. I knew my son. He had already overcome incredible odds just surviving his gestation, birth, and first two months in the neonatal intensive care unit. I just knew this would not be his story. I refused to claim it or speak it over him.

My little man and me—just the two of us—worked, worked, and then we worked some more. We did exercises multiple times throughout the day. Every time he was on the floor, I pushed his right knee up under him to force him into a proper crawling position. Despite his older sisters' busy schedules, my baby boy and I never missed a physical or occupational therapy appointment. It was difficult work and led to very fussy afternoons, but we persevered. And oh, how this mama prayed. I prayed Scripture over him and recounted the numerous ways God had already shown His faithfulness and provision in my son's life. I claimed further victories in his life, by the grace of God and power of His son, Jesus.

A few short weeks after the physical therapist spoke a future over my son that would leave him confined to a wheelchair, my son crawled. And just a few days later, he *walked*. He has been *running* full speed ever since. You should see the track ribbons on his wall! My friends, that is what we call victory.

Psalm 20
For the director of music. A psalm of David.
May the LORD answer you when you are in distress;
may the name of the God of Jacob protect you.
May he send you help from the sanctuary
and grant you support from Zion.
May he remember all your sacrifices
and accept your burnt offerings.
May he give you the desire of your heart
and make all your plans succeed.
May we shout for joy over your victory

and lift up our banners in the name of our God.
May the LORD *grant all your requests.*
Now this I know:
The LORD *gives victory to his anointed.*
He answers him from his heavenly sanctuary
with the victorious power of his right hand.
Some trust in chariots and some in horses,
but we trust in the name of the LORD *our God.*
They are brought to their knees and fall,
but we rise up and stand firm.
LORD, *give victory to the king!*
Answer us when we call!

Now, that is a battle cry! Looking back, the first two years with my son look like an unraveling and straightening out of damage that was done in his first critical months of life. He was a champion warrior! What my sweet boy needed from us was prayer, love, nurturing, time, and the expertise of various specialists to help him win his battles. And isn't that what we all need from time to time? Life can do a number on us, and when it does, we need time, love, someone to believe in us, and guidance. There is no shame in asking for help.

One of the most-named women in the Bible, Mary Magdalene, must have also asked for help. We know because of passages in Luke, chapter 8, that Mary had been healed of possession from seven demons. It's just my opinion, but I don't think all that healing would have happened had she not asked for help with what plagued her. After her miraculous healing, Mary traveled with Jesus and His disciples, supporting His ministry.

I remember praying that if my son, who was a foster child at the time, could just be ours, we would tell everyone that would listen of the ways God saved and provided for him and our family, just as Mary did. In pure, victorious, God-like fashion, that sick baby boy not only became ours, but he overcame multiple serious illnesses and hospitalizations, developmental issues, gastrointestinal deficiencies, asthma, and food allergies. He is a walking, living, breathing, talking *miracle*. People who meet him today have no clue of his past or even that he is adopted. From looking at him now, no one would ever suspect the difficulties he has had to overcome. God had plans for him!

Victory comes in all shapes and sizes. For many, victory is what they manage to accomplish despite the odds. For others, victory comes in *not* doing something, like not eating that dessert, not taking a sip of that alcohol, or not spreading that juicy bit of gossip. God resides in both the doing and the not doing. He can propel us forward toward our dreams and simultaneously help us abstain from that which may prevent us from reaching them.

It is in our weakness that we realize God's power and provision. When we are unable, He is able. When we are weak, He is strong. Where we see failure, He sees opportunity. Even when we lose, God ultimately and always wins.

> Even when we lose, God ultimately and always wins.

The Lord is my strength and my defense;
he has become my salvation.
Shouts of joy and victory resound in the tents of the
righteous:
"The Lord's right hand has done mighty things!
The Lord's right hand is lifted high;
the Lord's right hand has done mighty things!"
(Ps. 118:14–16)

Jesus Christ is the victory—over death, over evil, over this world, over our very own lives. Victory is His, and by believing in Him, victory is also ours.

FACING MINISTRY

*It is no use walking anywhere to preach
unless our walking is our preaching.*[57]
—St. Francis of Assisi

W e have a bedtime routine in our home and pray
together before heading to our bedrooms for the
night. One particular school night, after we gathered to
pray, I suddenly realized I had forgotten to make the kids'
lunches for school the next day. My preschool-aged son
quickly offered, "I'll make mine, Mommy! Ima make a pb
and j!" We said our prayers, and knowing it was bedtime,
I questioned allowing my son to come into the kitchen
to make his sandwich. I knew he would make a mess.
I knew I would have to clean it up. I knew the entire
process would delay us both getting to sleep. I knew I
could do it faster and better on my own. But he was so
darn excited to help, and not wanting to squelch that
desire, I said "OK, buddy, let's make your lunch."

We gathered bread, peanut butter, jelly, a butter knife,
and paper towels from the pantry. Then, I hoisted my
little boy up onto the counter. I started to open the peanut
butter when he yelled, "No Mommy! I do it!" I backed
away and gave him free rein. I busied myself, making
his sisters' lunches, and watched out of the corner of my

eye as he jammed the knife deep into the peanut butter, pulled it out, licked it, clumsily spread it on the bread in giant clumps, licked the knife again, redeposited it into the peanut butter, and repeated the process over and over—never forgetting to slobber all over the knife, might I add.

When he was satisfied with his creation, I congratulated him on a job well done. "You did such a great job," I said, "that I'm going to let this jar of peanut butter be *Johnathan's* jar from now on. It's *all yours!*" He was incredibly proud. We washed his hands and I tucked him into bed, then returned to the kitchen to quietly clean up the peanut butter slime from the counter, faucet, and sink.

The entire scenario reminded me of my relationship with ministry. You see, God doesn't need me to carry out ministry for Him, just like I didn't need my son to make his sandwich. My feeble attempts at sharing my gifts to further His kingdom probably makes a mess more often than not, and God could definitely accomplish His purposes faster and better on His own. But just like I wanted my son to learn to make a sandwich, and just like I wanted to share that precious time with him, God wants to spend time with me and teach me lessons as well. He allows me to join Him in the work He wants to do here simply because He wants to spend time with me and teach me about Himself. God's purposes will be accomplished with or without my so-called help. Outcomes are God's responsibility; obedience is mine. My job is to speak

God's purposes will be accomplished with or without my so-called help. Outcomes are God's responsibility; obedience is mine.

out—in words and actions—that which He has deposited within me.

In reality, the same is true for all of us because we are all in ministry in some form or fashion. Others are watching us and learning from us, whether we are intentional about our teaching or not. I love this familiar saying: You may be the only Bible some people will ever read. One of the ways I'm currently ministering is through writing this book. Many times, I have "needed" to be doing other things instead of typing away on this laptop. At this exact moment, I feel torn by my desire to plan supper, wash dishes, put away clean laundry, and haul Christmas boxes to the attic. In addition to this new book-writing ministry, God has also brought a wonderful young woman into my life with whom I have entered into a mentoring relationship. We meet at least once a week, and I swear I'm gaining twice as much from her as I'm giving in exchange. Still, I am ministering to her.

In the midst of both of these new ministries, I continue to serve as a worship leader, but I'm suddenly questioning that last calling. It's not that I feel God telling me to stop that ministry, but I'm also not feeling as compelled to do it as I once did. Is this because I am actively pursuing new ministries and feeling a rush of adrenaline and passion for them? Is it because God has called me to these new tasks, and therefore it is time to let go of my ministry as a worship leader?

Honestly, I don't have answers to these questions right now. I am pressing into God in prayer, seeking Him in quiet time and study, seeking counsel from elders and those closest to me, and waiting for direction. My sweet, new, mentored friend prayed over me this morning and asked God to "make my thoughts like His" concerning these ministry decisions. What a profound way of asking for discernment!

*"For my thoughts are not your thoughts, neither are your
ways my ways," declares the Lord. "As the heavens are
higher than the earth, so are my ways higher than your ways
and my thoughts than your thoughts."
(Isa. 55:8–9)*

As we seek direction from the Lord about how He
wants us to serve Him, so much of our struggle comes
from not thinking as He does. I know I worry about
situations that may never arise, people's reactions that
may never come, and feelings that may never surface. I
fret over missing out, while God has an even better future
planned than I can't even imagine. I forget that if God
calls me to something, then He will also equip me for it.
And He will reward my smallest act of obedience with
tenfold blessing.

I once enjoyed the leadership of a pastor named Judi
Mayne, and I am remembering now some words she
spoke to me many years ago: When your life is busy and
full with family and ministry, and God calls you to do
something new, know that He is also calling you to let go
of something old. You can't just keep adding more and
more to your plate. God won't ask you to do that.

God knows what and how much we can handle, and
He won't ask us for more than we can give. He does
ask a great deal, though! He asks just enough of us that
we have to rely heavily on Him to accomplish it. In this
way, we know it is not by our own strength that we
have completed His task, but by the Holy Spirit working
through us.

*Such confidence we have through Christ before God.
Not that we are competent in ourselves to claim
anything for ourselves, but our competence comes
from God. He has made us competent as ministers of*

*a new covenant—not of the letter but of the Spirit;
for the letter kills, but the Spirit gives life.
(2 Cor. 3:4–6)*

Ministry isn't convenient. It isn't easy. And if it doesn't cost us something, it isn't worth much.

Sound shocking? Consider Jesus. His ministry cost Him *everything*—His reputation, many of His friends, His very life. He knows the magnitude of what He is asking when He tells us to follow Him.

*Then he called the crowd to him along with his disciples and said: "Whoever wants to be my disciple must deny themselves and take up their cross and follow me. For whoever wants to save their life will lose it, but whoever loses their life for me and for the gospel will save it."
(Mark 8:34–35)*

Ministry isn't convenient. It isn't easy. And if it doesn't cost us something, it isn't worth much.

Deny yourself. Carry a cross. Lose your life. Follow. These aren't half-hearted, lukewarm sentiments. They also don't sound like the advice of most self-help / self-empowerment books these days. When it comes to ministry, Jesus wants us all in, just as He was all in. And that means checking "self" at the door.

News flash: it's not about us. The sole purpose of ministry is to communicate the message of the Gospel to others. How, what, when, and where God uses us to accomplish that will look different for everyone, but the *why* is clear. It's crucial we enter periods of discernment, as I am in the midst of now, so we can find clarity on the hows, whats, whens, and wheres God has planned for us.

Regardless of specifics, we are called—we are *all* called—
to minister and proclaim the Gospel.

> *Therefore go and make disciples of all nations,*
> *baptizing them in the name of the Father and of the*
> *Son and of the Holy Spirit, and teaching them to obey*
> *everything I have commanded you. And surely I am*
> *with you always, to the very end of the age.*
> *(Matt. 28:19–20)*

Remember, outcomes are His, and obedience is ours.
What a comfort to know we are not alone as we seek to
minister to others and serve the Lord!

FACING LEGACY

And I, I don't want to leave a legacy
I don't care if they remember me
Only Jesus
And I, I've only got one life to live
I'll let every second point to Him
Only Jesus[58]
—"Only Jesus" by Casting Crowns

Something beautiful is happening this fall. My husband and I decided to attend a Bible study at our church on Wednesday nights while our kids are attending youth activities. On our first night of study, I looked across the room and saw my father and stepmother. I crossed the room to hug them and asked which study they were starting that night, and they said they were staying for the same study my husband and I had chosen. Now, once a week, I get to sit down with my parents and other members of my church family and enjoy a meal and fellowship together, and then we take out our Bibles and notepads and dive in to Scripture under the leadership of our senior pastor.

Last night, I looked over to my right and saw my father's familiar but now aging hands, highlighting verses in his Bible as the pastor taught. It filled me with all kinds of gratitude for:

- these moments studying the word of God with my father and with the woman who helped raise me after my mother's death;
- a church family that loves and accepts me and others just as we are;
- a pastor who works diligently in His own life to model Jesus, and then leads us to do the same;
- a husband who seeks the Lord by my side; and
- the example of my father—a humble, hard-working, dependable, gentle, loyal man who loves deeply.

Is there anything sweeter than the privilege of learning about our heavenly Father through the example of our earthly father? I recognize the incalculable blessing my father has been and continues to be in my life. Not only an example to me, he now imparts the gifts of his love and wisdom to my own children, which serves to magnify my love for him and recognize his legacy even more. In a world where quality paternal role models are increasingly difficult to find, my father holds unswervingly to biblical ideals of the great responsibility of fathers and husbands.

Our legacies are the things we leave behind when we die, an inheritance of sorts for those who come after us. When I think of legacies, I think of my mother and father and grandparents, and the legacies of faith and examples of marriage and parenting they left for my sister and me. Growing up, I never felt they were pushing anything on me, only that I was deeply loved, safe, and cared for by both them and God above.

Have you ever thought about the legacy you want to leave? What do you want to be remembered for? When

I think of the legacy I am leaving, I think of this book in your hands, and my children. I want to pass on the lessons I have learned in my own life to others. I want my children to live godly lives that make the world around them better. Above all else, I want my legacy to point to Jesus. If I accomplish nothing else, I want to help others know the love and salvation I've found in Jesus Christ. I don't have all the answers. I don't get it right all the time, or even most of the time. And that is precisely why I rely on the only perfect one the world has even known.

> **Above all else, I want my legacy to point to Jesus.**

One of my favorite contemporary Christian songs by Big Daddy Weave says it like this:

If I told you my story
You would hear Hope that wouldn't let go
And if I told you my story
You would hear Love that never gave up
And if I told you my story
You would hear Life, but it wasn't mine
If I should speak then let it be
Of the grace that is greater than all my sin
Of when justice was served and where mercy wins
Of the kindness of Jesus that draws me in
Oh to tell you my story is to tell of Him[59]

You see, nothing this world claims I have done was really "me" anyway. I can't even draw a breath without God giving it to me first. These words? All Jesus. When I sing? Totally Jesus. When I offer kindness, exhibit self-control, or forgive someone? Definitely Jesus. When I speak gently and hug the child that has tested the ever-loving-snot out of me all day long? Thank you, baby Jesus, that is all You.

The only legacy I want to leave is the name of Jesus Christ. I don't care if you remember *me*. Only Jesus.

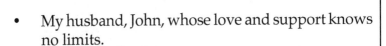

Acknowledgments

- My husband, John, whose love and support knows no limits.
- My children: Rachel, Grace, and Johnathan, who are my biggest cheerleaders. Special thanks to Johnathan, who agreed to being the brunt of many jokes for the sake of this book.
- My sister, Kristi Giles, who knows me like no one else does and loves me all the same. Special thanks for sharing her gifts for editing and brainstorming with me.
- My daddy, Jerry Dechert, whose encouragement and pride propels me onward and whose daily walk with Jesus inspires me.
- The educators who taught me that God gave me a gift with words, who lit a passion within me to express myself through the written word and who taught me the fine art of writing and editing: Louise Homilius, Barbara Wise, and Chris Bradley.
- Author and friend, Scott Delaney, who gave me priceless advice, direction, and introductions. Thank you so much!
- My very first editors: Kristi, Lori, Marla, Charlotte, Elizabeth, DeeAnn, and Steven. Thank you.

- My team at Xulon Press, particularly Kim Small, who put up with my many questions and successfully put this book in your hands. I am forever grateful.
- My friends in faith that shared their own gifts to make me look better: Jodi Carpenter (photography), Erin Dean (hair), and Leah Westra (makeup).
- You, dear reader, for supporting this ministry. May the words I have written—the meditations of my heart—be a blessing to you.

Notes

Facing Grief

1   Ed Sheeran, "Supermarket Flowers," ÷, Asylum Records, Atlantic Recording Co., 2018.

Facing Failure

2   Henry Ford. "My Life and Work." *Quote Investigator.* Accessed August 4, 2021. https://quoteinvestigator.com/2016/01/20/begin-again/.

Facing Unfairness

3   Oscar Wilde. "Oscar Wilde Quotes." *BrainyQuote.* https://www.brainyquote.com/quotes/oscar_wilde_121773, accessed August 4, 2021.

4   Rick Warren, *The Purpose-Driven Life* (Grand Rapids: Zondervan, 2002), 193–196.

5   Ryan Frederick. "Fierce Marriage." *Christian Marriage Quotes.* Accessed August 4, 2021. https://christianmarriagequotes.com/2157-grace-is-getting-what-you-dont-deserve-mercy-is-not-getting-what-you-do-deserve-a-joyful-marriage-requires-a-generous-portion-of-both/.

Facing Self-Scrutiny

6   Kiala Settle and The Greatest Showman Ensemble, "This is Me," *The Greatest Showman: Original Motion Picture Soundtrack*, Atlantic, 2017.

7   Lauren Daigle, "You Say," *Look Up Child*, Centricity, Warner Bros, 12Tone, 2018.

8   Ruth Chou Simons, *Gracelaced: Discovering Timeless Truths Through Seasons of the Heart* (Eugene: Harvest House Publishers, 2017), 82.

9   Jennifer Rothschild, *Me Myself & Lies* (Nashville: Lifeway Press, 2008), 23–26

10 Jennifer Rothschild, *Me Myself & Lies*, 24–26

Facing Disappointment

11 Bethel Music, Jonathan David Helser, Melissa Helser, "Raise a Hallelujah," *Victory*, Bethel Music, 2019.

Facing Trauma

12 Laura Story, "Blessings," *Blessings*, INO, 2011.

Facing Fear

13 Bethel Music, Jonathan David Helser, Melissa Helser, "No Longer Slaves," *We Will Not Be Shaken*, Bethel Music, 2015.

14 Craig Groeschel. Twitter Post. March 5, 2018, 7:00 a.m. https://twitter.com/craiggroeschel/status/970645195971809287?lang=en

Facing Terror

15 Alison Broussard and Mark Swayze Band, "Psalm 91," *This Album Feeds Children*, Alletrop Music, 2012.

16 Brené Brown. "Brené Brown: America's Crisis of Disconnection Runs Deeper than Politics." *Fast Company*. Accessed August 4, 2021. https://www.fastcompany.com/40465644/brene-brown-americas-crisis-of-disconnection-runs-deeper-than-politics.

17 Fred (Mister) Rogers. "64 Mister Rogers Quotes That Will Make Today a Beautiful Day." *Parade*. Accessed August 4, 2021. https://parade.com/954616/alexandra-hurtado/mr-rogers-quotes/.

Facing Sin

18 Elevation Worship. "O Come to the Altar," *Here as in Heaven*, Elevation, 2017.

Facing Everyday Life

19 Robert Earl Keen. "The Road Goes on Forever," *West Textures*, Sugar Hill, 1989.

20 Christine Caine. "Christine Caine Quotes and Sayings." *inspiringquotes.us*. Accessed August 5, 2021. https://www.inspiringquotes.us/author/3505-christine-caine.

Facing Weakness

21 Craig Roeschel. Twitter Post. December 30, 2018, 6:36 a.m. https://twitter.com/craiggroeschel/status/1079355425361936385?lang=en.

Facing Change

22 John F. Kennedy. "Address in the Assembly Hall at the Paulskirche in Frankfurt (266)," June 25, 1963, *Public Papers of the Presidents: John F. Kennedy, 1963*. Accessed August 5, 2021 on *John F. Kennedy Presidential Library and Museum*. https://www.jfklibrary.org/learn/about-jfk/life-of-john-f-kennedy/john-f-kennedy-quotations#C

Facing Emptiness

23 Caedmon's Call. "This World," *Caedmon's Call*, Warner Alliance, 1997.

Facing Prayer

24 Hillary Scott and the Scott Family. "Thy Will," *Love Remains*, EMI Nashville, Capitol Nashville, 2016.

Facing Misunderstanding

25 Margaret Elizabeth Sangster. "Margaret Elizabeth Sangster Quotes." *BrainyQuotes*. Accessed August 5, 2021. https://www.brainyquote.com/authors/margaret-elizabeth-sangst-quotes.

Facing Family

26 George Bernard Shaw. "George Bernard Shaw Quotes." *BrainyQuote*. Accessed August 5, 2021. https://www.brainyquote.com/search_results?x=0&y=0&q=george+bernard+shaw.

Facing Worry

27 Erma Bombeck. "Erma Bombeck Quotes About Life, Marriage and God." *EVERYDAYPOWER*. Accessed

August 5, 2021. https://everydaypower.com/erma-bombeck-quotes/.

Facing Doubt

28 Laura Story, "Blessings," *Blessings*, INO, 2011.

29 Don Henley. "The Heart of the Matter," *The End of the Innocence*, Geffen, 1988.

Facing Release

30 Oprah Winfrey. "Oprah Winfrey Quotes." *goodreads*. Accessed August 5, 2021. https://www.goodreads.com/quotes/62254-breathe-let-go-and-remind-yourself-that-this-very-moment.

Facing Love

31 Steven Curtis Chapman, "Love Take Me Over," *The Glorious Unfolding*, Reunion, 2013.

Facing Joy

32 Helen Keller. "*Out of the Dark: Essays, Lectures, and Addresses on Physical and Social Vision.*" Accessed August 5, 2021 on *AZ Quotes*. https://www.azquotes.com/quote/553535.

33 Ruth Chou Simons. *Beholding and Becoming: The Art of Everyday Worship* (Eugene: Harvest House, 2019), 34.

Facing Peace

34 Horatio Spafford. "Horatio Spafford." *Wikipedia*. Accessed August 5, 2021. https://en.wikipedia.org/wiki/Horatio_Spafford

Facing Patience

35 Dr. Seuss, *Oh! The Places You'll Go* (New York: Random House, 1990).

36 Bethel Music and Kristene DeMarco, "Take Courage," *Starlight*, Bethel, 2017.

37 Eric Johnson. Pastor at Bethel Church. Personal notes taken from a talk he gave on June 12, 2017, in Austin, Texas, at a Bethel Worship Nights tour date.

38 Ruth Chou Simons, *Gracelaced: Discovering Timeless Truths Through Seasons of the Heart* (Eugene: Harvest House Publishers, 2017), 171.

Facing Kindness

39 Fred (Mister) Rogers. "64 Mister Rogers Quotes That Will Make Today a Beautiful Day." *Parade*. Accessed August 5, 2021. https://parade.com/954616/alexandra-hurtado/mr-rogers-quotes/.

40 Fred (Mister) Rogers. "64 Mister Rogers Quotes That Will Make Today a Beautiful Day." *Parade*. Accessed August 5, 2021. https://parade.com/954616/alexandra-hurtado/mr-rogers-quotes/.

Facing Goodness

41 Robert Burns. "To a Mouse" by Robert Burns. *Poetry Foundation*. Accessed August 5, 2021. https://www.poetryfoundation.org/poems/43816/to-a-mouse-56d222ab36e33.

Facing Faithfulness

42 Chris Tomlin, "Whom Shall I Fear," *Burning Lights*, sixsteps, Sparrow, 2012.

Facing Gentleness

43 Saint Francis de Sales. "Wisdom from Saint Francis de Sales." *Oblates of Saint Francis de Sales.* Accessed August 5, 2021. https://www.oblates.org/st-francis-wisdom#practice-gentleness.

Facing Authenticity

44 The Evil Queen, "Snow White and the Seven Dwarfs," *Disney.* 1937.

45 Cigna. "New Cigna Study Reveals Loneliness at Epidemic Levels in America," *Cigna.* Accessed August 5, 2021. https://www.cigna.com/about-us/newsroom/news-and-views/press-releases/2018/new-cigna-study-reveals-loneliness-at-epidemic-levels-in-america.

Facing Spiritual Gifts

46 Taylor Swift. Twitter Post. May 10, 2014, 1:31 p.m. https://twitter.com/QuoteTaySwift/status/465197384356888578

Facing Identity

47 Fred (Mister) Rogers. "64 Mister Rogers Quotes That Will Make Today a Beautiful Day." *Parade.* Accessed August 5, 2021. https://parade.com/954616/alexandra-hurtado/mr-rogers-quotes/.

Facing Worship

48 Warren W. Wiersbe. "30 Great Quotes on Worship." *experiencing worship.* Accessed August 5, 2021. https://www.experiencingworship.com/articles/general/2001-7-great-quotes-on-worship.html.

49 Darlene Zschech. "Darlene Zschech quotes and sayings." *inspiringquotes.us.* Accessed August 5, 2021. https://www.inspiringquotes.us/author/4467-darlene-zschech.

50 Graham Kendrick. "Graham Kendrick Quotes." *A-Z Quotes.* Accessed August 5, 2021. https://www.azquotes.com/author/22503-Graham_Kendrick.

Facing Discipleship

51 Oswald Chambers. "Oswald Chambers Quotes About Discipleship." *inspiringquotes.us.* Accessed August 5, 2021. https://www.inspiringquotes.us/author/9496-oswald-chambers/about-discipleship.

Facing Contentment

52 Max Lucado. "*Cure for the Common Life: Living in Your Sweet Spot*" (Nashville: Thomas Nelson, 2005), 43.

53 Charles Spurgeon. "The 104 GREATEST, Most Profound Charles Spurgeon Quotes." *the blazing center.* Accessed August 5, 2021. https://theblazingcenter.com/2018/10/charles-spurgeon-quotes.html#contentment.

54 Max Lucado. "*Cure for the Common Life: Living in Your Sweet Spot*" (Nashville: Thomas Nelson, 2005), 3.

Facing Others

55 Albert Camus. "Albert Camus Quotes." *BrainyQuotes.* Accessed August 5, 2021. https://www.brainyquote.com/citation/quotes/albert_camus_378161.

Facing Victory

56 Warren W. Wiersbe. "Warren W. Wiersbe Quotes and Sayings." *inspiringquotes.us.* Accessed August 5 2021. https://www.inspiringquotes.us/author/6918-warren-w-wiersbe/page:2.

Facing Ministry

57 St. Francis of Assisi, quoted by Jamie Arpin-Ricci, "Preach the Gospel at all Times?" *HuffPost.* Accessed August 5, 2021. https://www.huffpost.com/entry/preach-the-gospel-at-all-times-st-francis_b_1627781.

Facing Legacy

58 Casting Crowns, "Only Jesus," *Only Jesus,* Beach Street, Reunion, Sony BMG, 2018.

59 Big Daddy Weave, "My Story," *Beautiful Offerings,* Word, Curb, Fervent, 2015.

CPSIA information can be obtained
at www.ICGtesting.com
Printed in the USA
LVHW021056021221
704799LV00004B/9